# Fresh Ways with
# Breakfasts and Brunches

*COVER*
*A light, nutrition-packed buffet brunch features fruit kebabs, scrambled egg cups with smoked salmon, and individual brioches baked from a dough made with less butter than the traditional version (recipes, pages 93, 122 and 40 respectively). Champagne blended with fresh orange juice and grape juice lends a sparkle (recipe, page 111).*

## TIME-LIFE BOOKS

EUROPEAN EDITOR: Ellen Phillips
*Design Director:* Ed Skyner
*Director of Editorial Resources:* Louise Tulip
*Chief Sub-Editor:* Ilse Gray

LOST CIVILIZATIONS
HOW THINGS WORK
SYSTEM EARTH
LIBRARY OF CURIOUS AND
UNUSUAL FACTS
BUILDING BLOCKS
A CHILD'S FIRST LIBRARY OF LEARNING
VOYAGE THROUGH THE UNIVERSE
THE THIRD REICH
MYSTERIES OF THE UNKNOWN
TIME-LIFE HISTORY OF THE WORLD
FITNESS, HEALTH & NUTRITION
HEALTHY HOME COOKING
UNDERSTANDING COMPUTERS
THE ENCHANTED WORLD
LIBRARY OF NATIONS
PLANET EARTH
THE GOOD COOK
THE WORLD'S WILD PLACES

ISBN 1 86019 081 2
TIME-LIFE is a trademark of Time Warner Inc. U.S.A.

## HEALTHY HOME COOKING

SERIES DIRECTOR: Dale M. Brown
*Series Administrators:* Jane Edwin, Elise Ritter Gibson
*Designer:* Tom Huetis
*Picture Editor:* Sally Collins
*Photographer:* Renée Comet
*Editorial Assistant:* Rebecca C. Christofferson

Editorial Staff for *Fresh Ways with Breakfasts & Brunches:*
*Book Managers:* Jean Getlin, Barbara Sause
*Associate Picture Editor:* Scarlet Cheng
*Assistant Designer:* Elissa E. Baldwin
*Researcher/Writers:* Henry Grossi, Susan Stuck
*Copy Coordinators:* Elizabeth Graham, Ruth Baja Williams
*Picture Coordinator:* Linda Yates
*Photographer's Assistant:* Mazyar Parvaresh
*Kitchen Assistant:* Chhomaly Sok

European Edition:
*Sub-Editor:* Wendy Gibbons
*Chief of Editorial Production:* Maureen Kelly
*Assistant:* Deborah Fulham
*Editorial Department:* Theresa John, Debra  Lelliott

## THE COOKS

LISA CHERKASKY has worked as a chef in Madison, Wisconsin, and in Washington, D.C. She is a graduate of the Culinary Institute of America.

ADAM DE VITO began his cooking apprenticeship when he was only 14. He has worked at Le Pavillon restaurant in Washington, D.C., taught with cookery author Madeleine Kamman, and conducted classes at L'Académie de Cuisine in Maryland.

JOHN T. SHAFFER is a graduate of The Culinary Institute of America. He has had broad experience as a chef, including five years at the Four Seasons Hotel in Washington, D.C.

## CONSULTANTS

CAROL CUTLER is the author of many cookery books. During the 12 years she lived in France, she studied at the Cordon Bleu and the École des Trois Gourmandes, as well as with private chefs. She is a member of the Cercle des Gourmettes and a charter member and past president of Les Dames D'Escoffier.

NORMA MACMILLAN has written several cookery books and edited many others. She has worked on various cookery publications, including *Grand Diplôme* and *Supercook*. She lives and works in London.

PAT ALBUREY, is a home economist with a wide experience of preparing foods for photography, teaching cookery and creating recipes. She has been involved in a number of cookery books and was the studio consultant for the Time-Life series *The Good Cook*.

## NUTRITION CONSULTANTS

JANET TENNEY has been involved in nutrition and consumer affairs since she received her master's degree in human nutrition from Columbia University. She is the manager for developing and implementing nutritional programmes for a major chain of supermarkets.

PATRICIA JUDD trained as a dietician and worked in hospital practice before returning to university to obtain her MSc and PhD degrees. Since then she has lectured in Nutrition and Dietetics at London University.

Nutritional analyses for *Fresh Ways with Breakfasts & Brunches* were derived from Practorcare's Nutriplanner System and other current data.

This volume is one of a series of illustrated cookery books that emphasize the preparation of healthy dishes for today's weight-conscious, nutrition-minded eaters.

# Fresh Ways with Breakfasts and Brunches

BY

THE EDITORS OF TIME-LIFE BOOKS

# Contents

*Orange, Grapefruit and Honeydew Melon with Port*

*Chilled Papaya Shake*

*Turkey, Apple and Champagne Patties*

Chinese Brunch

# Good Beginnings

The first meal of the day has an emotional aura quite unlike that of any other meal. Perhaps this springs from our peculiar vulnerability in the morning, when we still have sleep in our eyes and are feeling a little fuzzy, in need of gentle handling and a shock-free passage from the world of dreams into the world of reality. Presumably we also need nourishment to restore us after our long night's fast. The morning meal, more than lunch or dinner, reminds us of the essential function of food: to fuel our bodies.

When most of us think of breakfast, just a handful of foods and beverages come to mind. These tend to be bland, safe, comfortingly familiar to the point of being boring: orange juice, grapefruit, bananas or prunes, cereals, eggs, bacon or sausage, toast or rolls, milk, coffee, tea. Added to this are foods typical of particular countries: cheese, bread, ham, boiled eggs in Germany; croissants or bread and jam in France, served with a large cup of *café au lait;* waffles or pancakes and maple syrup in America; and, of course, our own porridge, bacon and eggs, kippers, and toast and marmalade.

In other parts of the world, breakfast is a far more eclectic affair. The Japanese think nothing of having soup upon arising. An Egyptian finds a bowl of beans as appropriate in the morning as in the evening. And a Chinese will happily down steamed or fried rice and a variety of dumplings, known as *dim sum —* "things that touch the heart".

Brunch — another, more elaborate way of breaking our daily fast — takes a liberalized approach to morning eating. A cross between breakfast and lunch, brunch piques imaginations — and appetites — because it is distinctly out of the ordinary daily routine. Timing alone makes brunch an innately festive meal: usually meant to begin somewhere between 11 a.m. and 1 p.m., it is a meal for Sundays or holidays or the special Saturday when weekend chores are set aside and guests or family can be leisurely entertained.

This book takes its cue from brunch's freedom and reinvigorates morning eating with 130 original recipes. And it does so with your health in mind. It minimizes fats and salt, keeps protein in

balance and maximizes fibre and complex carbohydrates, present in fruits, grains and vegetables.

Although not all nutritionists believe that breakfast is actually a requirement for a healthy eating style, they generally agree that the meal is typically a matter of unhealthy extremes. There are many people, of course, who eat literally nothing for hours after arising; they effectively prolong the fast of the night to 12 or 15 hours or even longer. Some adults who follow this pattern get on quite well with their morning's activities. But for children, going without breakfast is another matter. Studies show that children who have had breakfast perform much better in school; they are less listless and can concentrate more effectively on their tasks.

In any case, eating a morning meal appears to make sound biological sense: anthropologists think that our early ancestors were habitual nibblers who, in effect, ate many small meals through the day as they came upon edible berries, fruits or roots. Laboratory studies suggest that people may live longer when they eat three or more meals a day. Experiments with animals indicate that the animals fed one or two large meals gain twice as much body fat as those given the same number of calories divided among more frequent meals. Though the evidence is not clear-cut for humans, many nutritionists believe that eating breakfast does help control weight. Those persons who skip breakfast — or eat very little upon waking — may capitulate to fattening mid-morning snacks or be so ravenous by lunchtime that they overeat.

Nutritionists recommend that breakfast provide a quarter of the day's calories — some 500 for the average woman and 675 for a man. By telescoping two meals into one, brunch can account for an even bigger bite — 800 calories for a woman and 1,080 for a man. The brunch menus and recipes in this volume have been developed to take these maximums into account, and to provide as much as 40 per cent of the day's calories.

While most people do not skip breakfast, many eat a breakfast so bereft of nutrition that they need almost not bother. A sweet bun, consumed with a cup of coffee, will be high in calories, fat, and sugar, to be sure, but fail to assuage appetite for long. Sugar's simple carbohydrates are quickly absorbed, and instead of a steady flow of energy to keep the body running smoothly through the morning, the level of blood sugar — the form in which energy is supplied to the body's cells — rises sharply to a peak, then declines rapidly, soon to be followed by a gnawing in the pit of the stomach. By contrast, complex carbohydrates are digested slowly, so that they provide a gradual and sustained level of blood sugar that forestalls hunger.

At the opposite extreme is the traditional fried breakfast. With its sausages, bacon, eggs, jams and buttery breads, it is undesirably weighted with cholesterol, sugar and fat, as well as too much protein.

## Getting it right

Like lunch and dinner, the good breakfast should strike a balance between the different categories of food. Ideally, about 60 or 65 per cent of breakfast's calories should come from complex carbohydrates, 20 to 25 per cent from fats, another 10 per cent from protein, and the remaining 5 per cent or less from sugar, syrup or honey. Weight for weight, proteins and carbohydrates contain less than half the calories of fat.

Foods that are loaded with complex carbohydrates are said to be nutritionally dense, since they also contain vitamins, minerals and protein. Invariably these foods contain little or no fat. Often the little fat present is of the unsaturated variety that, unlike the saturated fat found in meat, eggs, milk, cream and cheese, has not been implicated in heart disease or other circulatory disorders.

Because they are such a rich source of complex carbohydrates, grains and vegetables are used frequently in the recipes making up this book. You will find these foods served up in tempting variations of traditional dishes, as well as in delicious innovations that can sway the most confirmed breakfast-hater.

## Breads of all kinds

No breakfast or brunch would be complete without bread in one form or another — yeast-raised loaves, unleavened flatbreads, muffins, dumplings, buns. Among the breads offered here, some are sweet, some savoury, some baked, others steamed or cooked quickly on a griddle.

For sound health reasons, many of the recipes call for whole grains. Since these have been given only the lightest milling, just enough to strip the inedible outer husk from the kernel, they retain all three edible parts of the kernel: the fibre-rich jacket of bran; the starchy endosperm, which accounts for about 80 per cent of the kernel's weight; and, enclosed by the endosperm, the germ. It is the germ that gives whole grains their distinctive,

rather nutty flavour, as well as their B and E vitamins and protein; the bran supplies the fibre.

Whole grains are marketed in a variety of forms. Groats are the coarsest — they are simply the whole kernel, minus its husk. Buckwheat, oats and wheat (somewhat inaccurately, the wheat groat is called a berry) can be purchased in groat form. Groats are also cracked or sliced into small pieces, or ground into flour or meal of varying degrees of fineness.

Because they retain the oil-laden germ, whole-grain products are much quicker to spoil than more highly refined products. Plain flour will keep up to six months at room temperature. Stored in a tightly covered container in the refrigerator, groats remain fresh for four to five months. The more finely textured products, including cracked wheat, meal and flour, are quicker to spoil. Buy them in small quantities, store them in the refrigerator, and plan to use them within three months.

Several of the breads in this book call for combinations of different flours. Where a light texture is desirable, it is essential to include a large portion of flour milled from wheat. Only wheat contains a significant amount of gluten, the protein that gives bread its structure. Plain white flour produces a lighter-textured bread than wholemeal flour, whose germ and bran content interfere with the gluten's ability to develop fully. Strong white flour has more gluten and creates a sturdier loaf.

Thorough kneading is essential to provide a yeast-leavened dough with good body. But quick breads, which generally are leavened by bicarbonate of soda or baking powder, actually suffer if they are mixed too long or too vigorously. Bicarbonate of soda and baking powder, like yeast organisms, release bubbles of carbon dioxide that cause dough to rise. But whereas yeast tends to work slowly, these agents go into action as soon as they are moistened. Consequently, quick bread batters or doughs should be mixed only long enough to combine the ingredients well — overmixing will drive out the carbon dioxide bubbles.

Do not let a quick bread dough or batter stand for long after mixing, since delaying cooking will allow the carbon dioxide to escape. Once the bread is done, serve it warm or as fresh as possible; it will not benefit from standing around any more than would a griddle cake or a waffle.

Keep your baking powder tightly covered and discard the unused portion no more than 12 months after purchase —otherwise you risk disappointing results. You can test baking powder's efficacy by adding 1 teaspoon to 6 tablespoons of hot water. Few bubbles mean that the baking powder is past its prime.

The quick breads most closely identified with breakfast and brunch are griddle cakes, waffles and French toast. As conventionally prepared, they tend to be high in calories, fat and cholesterol; for this book, they have all been redesigned to fit a healthier mould. Egg yolks have been reduced in the recipes (a

## The Key to Better Eating

Healthy Home Cooking addresses the concerns of today's weight-conscious, health-minded cooks with recipes that take into account guidelines set by nutritionists. The secret to eating well, of course, has to do with maintaining a balance of foods in the diet. The recipes thus should be used thoughtfully, in the context of a day's eating. To make the choice easier, this book presents an analysis of nutrients in a single serving of each breakfast and brunch recipe, as in the breakdown on the right. The counts for calories, protein, cholesterol, total fat, saturated fat and sodium are approximate.

### Interpreting the chart

The chart below gives dietary guidelines for healthy men, women and children. Recommended figures vary from country to country, but the principles are the same everywhere. Here, the average daily amounts of calories and protein are from a report by the U.K. Department of Health and Social Security; the maximum advisable daily intake of fat is based on guidelines given by the National Advisory Committee on Nutrition Education (NACNE); those for cholesterol and sodium are based on upper limits suggested by the World Health Organization.

The volumes in the Healthy Home Cooking series do not purport to be diet books, nor do they focus on health foods. Rather, they express a commonsense approach to cooking that uses salt, sugar, cream, butter and oil in moderation while employing other ingredients that also provide flavour and satisfaction. Herbs, spices and aromatic vegetables, as well as fruits, peels, juices, wines and vinegars, are all used towards this end.

In this volume, both safflower oil and virgin olive oil are called for. Safflower oil was chosen because it is the most highly polyunsaturated vegetable fat available in supermarkets and polyunsaturated fats reduce blood cholesterol. Virgin olive oil is used because it has a fine fruity flavour that is lacking in the lesser grade known as "pure". In

---

Calories **110**
Protein **14g**
Cholesterol **30mg**
Total fat **2g**
Saturated fat **1g**
Sodium **165mg**

---

addition, virgin olive oil is — like all olive oil — high in monounsaturated fats, which are thought not to increase blood cholesterol. Some cooks, seeking a still fruitier flavour for their brunchtime salads, may wish to use extra virgin olive oil or even extra extra virgin, although the price will, of course, be higher, reflecting the quality of such an oil.

The recipes make few unusual demands. Naturally they call for fresh ingredients, offering substitutes when these are unavailable. (The substitute is not calculated in the analysis, however.) Most of the recipe ingredients can be found in any well-stocked supermarket. If whole grains are unavailable, look for them in a health food store. Any that may seem unusual are described in a glossary on pages 139 and 140. In those instances where particular techniques may

not be familiar to a cook, there are appropriate how-to photographs.

In Healthy Home Cooking's test kitchens, heavy-bottomed pots and pans are used to guard against burning the food whenever a small amount of oil is used and where there is the danger that the food will adhere to the hot surface, but non-stick pans can be utilized as well.

### About cooking times

To help the cook plan ahead, Healthy Home Cooking takes time into account in its recipes. While recognizing that everyone cooks at a different speed, and that stoves and ovens differ, the series provides approximate "working" and "total" times for every dish. Working time stands for the minutes actively spent on preparation; total time includes unattended cooking time, as well as time devoted to marinating or chilling ingredients. Since the recipes emphasize fresh foods, they may take a bit longer to prepare than "quick and easy" dishes that call for canned or packaged products, but the payoff in flavour, and often in nutrition, should compensate for the little extra time involved.

## Recommended Dietary Guidelines

| | | Average Daily Intake | | Maximum Daily Intake | | | |
|---|---|---|---|---|---|---|---|
| | | CALORIES | PROTEIN grams | CHOLESTEROL milligrams | TOTAL FAT grams | SATURATED FAT grams | SODIUM milligrams |
| Females | 7-8 | 1900 | 47 | 300 | 80 | 32 | 2000* |
| | 9-11 | 2050 | 51 | 300 | 77 | 35 | 2000 |
| | 12-17 | 2150 | 53 | 300 | 81 | 36' | 2000 |
| | 18-54 | 2150 | 54 | 300 | 81 | 36 | 2000 |
| | 54-74 | 1900 | 47 | 300 | 72 | 32 | 2000 |
| Males | 7-8 | 1980 | 49 | 300 | 80 | 33 | 2000 |
| | 9-11 | 2280 | 57 | 300 | 77 | 38 | 2000 |
| | 12-14 | 2640 | 66 | 300 | 99 | 44 | 2000 |
| | 15-17 | 2880 | 72 | 300 | 108 | 48 | 2000 |
| | 18-34 | 2900 | 72 | 300 | 109 | 48 | 2000 |
| | 35-64 | 2750 | 69 | 300 | 104 | 35 | 2000 |
| | 65-74 | 2400 | 60 | 300 | 91 | 40 | 2000 |

* (or 5g salt)

single yolk suffices for four people) and egg whites increased, with results that are light, moist and tender. The commercial syrups and spreads ordinarily served with these breads are replaced by home-made versions that are deliberately less sweet, yet full of natural fruit flavour. And fresh fruit is the basis of several delightful toppings.

The fat and caloric content of stove-top breads can be further reduced by the right choice of the pan or griddle. With a non-stick finish or, in the case of a cast-iron utensil, a well-seasoned cooking surface, only a trace of fat need be added to prevent the bread from sticking.

To season a cast-iron pan, cover its cooking surface with a flavourless vegetable oil. Place the pan in a 130°C (250°F or Mark ½) oven. After an hour, turn off the heat and leave the pan in the oven for 12 hours. When you remove the pan, wipe it with paper towels to remove any excess oil. To clean the pan after cooking without damaging the seasoning, simply rinse it with water, dry it and wipe it out lightly with a paper towel soaked with a little vegetable oil.

For most people, breakfast is not complete without a bracing cup of hot coffee or tea. Like the frying pan or griddle, the coffee pot deserves special attention. Even if you eschew coffee in favour of tea, cocoa, fruit juice or some other morning beverage, there may be times when you will want to serve a well-made brew. Since bare metal can impart a bitter flavour to coffee, choose a pot made of glass or porcelain and clean it after every use with a solution of bicarbonate of soda and water. (Soap or detergent may leave a residue or film.) And, whether you make coffee by filter, vacuum or percolator method, remove the grounds and serve the coffee immediately or, at the very latest, within half an hour of brewing it. If this is not possible, keep coffee warm over gentle heat; never allow it to boil — boiling will only make it bitter.

## How this book works

The recipes in the first section are for both breakfast and brunch dishes — hot cereals, baked breads, stove-top breads, beverages, side dishes of fruits or vegetables, spreads, and main dishes based on eggs, grains, meat or seafood. Some of these are good candidates for workday breakfasts, such as the speedily prepared frozen peach, banana and buttermilk drink on page 23 that is practically a meal in a glass.

The second section of the book offers a series of brunch menus that include main dishes, salads, soup, side dishes, light desserts, breads and beverages. Some of the menus take their inspiration from a particular national or regional culinary tradition, while others reflect a seasonal theme. There is, as well, a menu for a simple picnic brunch and another for a buffet suitable for a dozen people.

The third and last section features microwave recipes. When time is short, a microwave oven can be a tremendous help in getting breakfast or brunch on the table fast.

And time is a key issue. It is the reason that so many people make do with a breakfast that is a skimpy, unsatisfying, rushed affair. With a little planning and organization, however, it is possible to have an appetizing, healthy meal in the morning. For some people, of course, getting organized shortly after rising is not within their nature. Time set aside the night before for a few chores will help speed up operations in the morning. Steps that can be taken in advance are:
● Set the table and get out the utensils you will need.
● Measure and combine all the dry ingredients for stove-top breads, muffins or quick breads; cover them tightly so that no flavours or aromas will escape.
● Mix liquid ingredients for griddle cakes, French toast or waffles; cover the containers tightly and refrigerate them.
● Oil baking tins.

Although brunch, by virtue of its later hour, allows more morning preparation time, it is still wise to do some of the work at least a day ahead:
● Cook pancakes, stack them one upon another between pieces of greaseproof paper, wrap them tightly in foil and refrigerate them.
● Prepare frozen dishes such as sorbets or chilled ones such as moulded salads and soups.
● Bake biscuits and yeast breads. Most yeast breads actually benefit from being baked a day in advance, since their flavour will improve and their texture will become firmer, thus making them easier to slice.
● Cook and refrigerate seafood, covered, for use in salads or as filling for pancakes.
● Prepare sauces, toppings and spreads.
● Mix marinades and refrigerate them.
● Cook the base for a soufflé and refrigerate it. The next day, heat it gently before adding the other ingredients.

With some of the work done in advance, you will have more of an opportunity to be with your guests and to enjoy with them a meal that is not only delicious but good for them.

*1* *A leisurely but light breakfast in a sunlit conservatory features a fruit compote and a brioche loaf with pear butter.*

# Pleasures of Morning

Morning eating comes in many guises, and this section shows just how diverse and enjoyable it can be. You will find recipes for an array of breakfast and brunch dishes, some as predictable as griddle cakes (but with a difference), and others as surprising as a vegetable-stuffed phyllo roll *(page 83)*.

Because healthy eating means going easy on salt and fat, none of the prepared meats ordinarily linked with morning meals are included here. (Bacon alone consists of more than two thirds fat, and pork sausage is often half fat.) Instead, the recipes use low-fat protein sources: fish, poultry, ricotta cheese, yogurt, and extra-lean cuts of beef and pork. Typical of this approach is a home-made sausage of minced turkey, delicately laced with champagne to lend it a piquancy that more than makes up for the little salt used.

To give early morning eating a boost, the recipes involve enticing blends of flavours. Buttermilk, fruit and spices enliven whole-grain hot cereals, whose innately richer taste needs less bolstering with salt than the blander refined cereals. Similarly, spring onions, sage and dill bring a delightful accent to some of the other early-day dishes assembled here.

Fresh fruit has particular importance in morning menus. Frothy mixtures of fruit and milk make wonderful eye openers. Chopped and stirred into a batter for baked or stove-top breads, fruit satisfies the longing for something sweet at low caloric cost. In addition, there are several fruit dishes that can be prepared in a matter of minutes and are as suitable for a weekend brunch as a workday breakfast. Rounding out the fruit recipes are a variety of toppings, syrups and relishes. These fruity fillips have multiple uses. For instance, the strawberry-cranberry jam that accompanies the main dish turkey-cheese sandwich on page 68 is equally delicious paired with the orange French toast on page 63 or the cornmeal-buttermilk pancakes on page 61 — all dishes that should encourage you to rise and shine.

# Apple Muesli

THE TRADITIONAL SWISS MUESLI, ON WHICH THIS
RECIPE IS BASED, USUALLY CONTAINS DRIED FRUIT;
HERE FRESH FRUIT IS USED, AND THE CEREAL IS MOISTENED
WITH BOTH APPLE JUICE AND YOGURT

Serves 6
Working (and total) time: about 10 minutes

Calories **160**
Protein **5g**
Cholesterol **2mg**
Total fat **3g**
Saturated fat **0g**
Sodium **30mg**

| | | |
|---|---|---|
| 1 | red apple, quartered, cored and coarsely chopped | 1 |
| 1 | yellow apple, quartered, cored and coarsely chopped | 1 |
| 12.5 cl | unsweetened apple juice | 4 fl oz |
| 75 g | quick-cooking rolled oats | 2½ oz |
| 1 tbsp | honey | 1 tbsp |
| ¼ litre | plain low-fat yogurt | 8 fl oz |
| 2 tbsp | sliced almonds | 2 tbsp |
| 2 tbsp | raisins | 2 tbsp |
| 1 tbsp | dark brown sugar | 1 tbsp |

Put the chopped apples into a large bowl. Add the apple juice and toss the apples to moisten them. Stir in the oats and honey, then add the yogurt, almonds and raisins. Stir to combine the mixture well.

Serve the muesli in individual bowls; sprinkle each serving with ½ teaspoon of the brown sugar.

EDITOR'S NOTE: *If you wish, the muesli can be made ahead and kept in the refrigerator, covered with plastic film, for up to two days.*

# Granola

WITH MILK ADDED, THIS GRANOLA BECOMES
A BREAKFAST IN ITSELF.

Serves 8
Working (and total) time: about 30 minutes

Calories **255**
Protein **6g**
Cholesterol **0mg**
Total fat **10g**
Saturated fat **1g**
Sodium **100mg**

| | | |
|---|---|---|
| 75 g | rolled oats | 2½ oz |
| 25 g | wheat bran | ¾ oz |
| 30 g | untoasted sunflower seeds | 1 oz |
| 60 g | whole blanched almonds | 2 oz |
| 2 tbsp | sesame seeds | 2 tbsp |
| 2 tsp | safflower oil | 2 tsp |
| ¼ tsp | salt | ¼ tsp |
| 150 g | raisins | 5 oz |
| 10 | dates, stoned and chopped | 10 |
| 2 tbsp | honey | 2 tbsp |
| 1 tsp | pure vanilla extract | 1 tsp |
| 1 | orange, grated rind only | 1 |

Preheat the oven to 200°C (400°F or Mark 6). Combine the oats, bran, sunflower seeds, almonds, sesame seeds, oil and salt in a large bowl. Spread the mixture evenly on a baking tray and toast it in the oven, stirring the mixture every 5 minutes, until it is lightly browned — about 15 minutes.

Return the toasted mixture to the bowl. Stir in the raisins, dates, honey, vanilla extract and orange rind. Let the granola cool completely before storing it in an airtight container. Serve the granola in individual bowls, with semi-skimmed milk poured over it if you like.

# Apricot-Orange Breakfast Couscous

Serves 4
Working time: about 5 minutes
Total time: about 10 minutes

Calories **220**
Protein **6g**
Cholesterol **0mg**
Total fat **2g**
Saturated fat **1g**
Sodium **205mg**

| | | |
|---|---|---|
| ¼ litre | fresh orange juice | 8 fl oz |
| 12 | dried apricot halves, thinly sliced | 12 |
| ¼ tsp | salt | ¼ tsp |
| 175 g | couscous | 6 oz |
| 3 tbsp | shredded coconut | 3 tbsp |
| | fresh fruit (optional) | |
| | semi-skimmed milk (optional) | |

Put the orange juice, ¼ litre (8 fl oz) of water, all but 1 tablespoon of the apricots and the salt into a medium saucepan. Bring the mixture to the boil. Stir in the couscous and remove the pan from the heat; cover the pan and let it stand for 5 minutes.

Toast the coconut by putting it in a small, heavy saucepan and cooking it, stirring constantly, until it is lightly browned — about 5 minutes. Spoon the couscous into individual serving bowls. Top each portion with some of the reserved tablespoon of sliced apricot and some coconut. You may garnish the hot cereal with fresh fruit such as raspberries, orange segments, or sliced pineapple or mango. Serve the cereal at once; accompany it with semi-skimmed milk if you like.

## Apple-Cinnamon Breakfast Burghul

Serves 4
Working time: about 5 minutes
Total time: about 20 minutes

Calories **208**
Protein **5g**
Cholesterol **0mg**
Total fat **1g**
Saturated fat **0g**
Sodium **135mg**

| | | |
|---|---|---|
| 1 | tart apple, preferably Granny Smith, cut in half and cored | 1 |
| ¼ litre | unsweetened apple juice, plus 1 tbsp | 8 fl oz |
| 1 tbsp | currants or raisins | 1 tbsp |
| ¼ tsp | ground cinnamon | ¼ tsp |
| ¼ tsp | salt | ¼ tsp |
| 175 g | burghul | 6 oz |
| | semi-skimmed milk (optional) | |

Cut one half of the apple into thin slices. Put the apple slices into a small bowl and toss them with the 1 tablespoon of apple juice. Set the bowl aside.

Cut the remaining apple half into small chunks. Put the chunks into a heavy-bottomed saucepan. Add the remaining apple juice, ¼ litre (8 fl oz) of water, the currants or raisins, the cinnamon and the salt, and bring the mixture to the boil. Stir in the burghul, then cover the pan and reduce the heat to medium low. Simmer the burghul mixture until all of the liquid is absorbed — about 15 minutes.

Spoon the burghul into individual serving bowls and decorate with some of the reserved apple slices. If you like, serve the cereal with semi-skimmed milk.

# Toasted Brown Rice Cereal with Orange and Cocoa

Serves 6
Working time: about 15 minutes
Total time: about 30 minutes

Calories **215**
Protein **3g**
Cholesterol **0mg**
Total fat **10g**
Saturated fat **0g**
Sodium **100mg**

| | | |
|---|---|---|
| 175 g | brown rice | 6 oz |
| ¼ tsp | salt | ¼ tsp |
| 2 tbsp | unsweetened cocoa powder | 2 tbsp |
| 90 g | dark brown sugar | 3 oz |
| 12.5 cl | fresh orange juice | 4 fl oz |
| 1 | orange, peeled and cut into segments | 1 |

Toast the brown rice in a heavy frying pan over medium-high heat, shaking the pan occasionally, until the rice begins to crackle and some of the kernels start to burst — 7 to 10 minutes. Transfer the rice to a blender and grind it until it resembles coarse sand.

Put the ground rice and salt into a saucepan; add ¾ litre (1¼ pints) of cold water and bring the mixture to a simmer over medium-high heat. Reduce the heat to medium low, then cover the pan and cook the rice until all but about ¼ litre (8 fl oz) of the water has been absorbed and the rice is tender — approximately 15 minutes. Remove the pan from the heat. Sift the cocoa on to the rice and then stir it in. Add the brown sugar and orange juice; stir the mixture well.

Spoon the cereal into warm bowls, then top each serving with several of the orange segments. Serve the cereal with semi-skimmed milk, if you like.

## Multigrain Cereal Mix

THIS UNCOOKED CEREAL CAN BE AS VARIED OR SIMPLE AS
YOU LIKE. YOU MAY LEAVE OUT ONE OR TWO OF THE
GRAINS. MOST OF THE INGREDIENTS ARE READILY FOUND IN
THE SUPERMARKET. THE MILLET AND BROWN RICE FLAKES
ARE FOUND IN MOST HEALTH FOOD STORES.

Makes about 16 servings
Working (and total) time: about 10 minutes

Calories **100**
Protein **2g**
Cholesterol **0mg**
Total fat **1g**
Saturated fat **0g**
Sodium **25mg**

| | | |
|---|---|---|
| 75 g | rolled oats | 2½ oz |
| 15 g | puffed wheat | ½ oz |
| 75 g | millet flakes | 2½ oz |
| 100 g | brown rice flakes | 3½ oz |
| 100 g | wheat flakes | 3½ oz |
| 60 g | sultanas | 2 oz |
| 2 tbsp | chopped toasted hazelnuts | 2 tbsp |

Combine the cereals in a large bowl. Stir in the
sultanas and the chopped nuts.

Store the cereal mix in an airtight container. If you
wish, serve each portion with semi-skimmed milk or
low-fat yogurt.

EDITOR'S NOTE: *You may add 45 g (1½ oz) of chopped, stoned
dates or 1 tablespoon of toasted sunflower seeds to this
cereal. To toast the nuts or sunflower seeds, put them in a
heavy frying pan over medium-high heat and stir them constantly until they are lightly browned — 2 to 3 minutes.*

# Orange and Banana Porridge

Serves 4
Working (and total) time: about 10 minutes

Calories **195**
Protein **6g**
Cholesterol **1mg**
Total fat **2g**
Saturated fat **0g**
Sodium **17mg**

| | | |
|---|---|---:|
| 33 cl | fresh orange juice | 11 fl oz |
| 1 tsp | grated orange rind | 1 tsp |
| 1 | banana, coarsely chopped | 1 |
| 125 g | quick-cooking rolled oats | 4 oz |
| 12.5 cl | skimmed milk | 4 fl oz |
| 1 | orange, peeled and segmented | 1 |

Combine the orange juice, orange rind and banana in a non-reactive saucepan and bring the mixture to the boil. Stir in the rolled oats, reduce the heat to low and cook the mixture, covered, for 1 minute. Take the pan from the heat and let the porridge stand, covered, until it has thickened — about 1 minute more.

Spoon the cereal into four individual bowls; add 2 tablespoons of the milk to each bowl and garnish it with one or two of the orange segments. Serve the porridge at once.

## Mixed Vegetable Eye Opener

Makes 2 servings
Working time: about 20 minutes
Total time: about 1 hour (includes chilling)

Calories **65**
Protein **3g**
Cholesterol **0mg**
Total fat **0g**
Saturated fat **0g**
Sodium **210mg**

| | | |
|---|---|---|
| 2 | sticks celery, trimmed, leaves reserved | 2 |
| 1 | small cucumber, peeled, seeded and coarsely chopped | 1 |
| 1½ tsp | fresh lemon juice | 1½ tsp |
| 8 | drops Tabasco sauce | 8 |
| 400 g | canned whole tomatoes, seeded, with their juice | 14 oz |
| ⅛ tsp | salt | ⅛ tsp |
| ½ tsp | caster sugar | ½ tsp |
| 2 | spring onions, white parts only, coarsely chopped | 2 |
| ½ tsp | ground ginger | ½ tsp |
| ¼ tsp | dill seeds (optional) | ¼ tsp |
| 1 | carrot, quartered lengthwise, for garnish | 1 |

Remove the strings from the celery using a vegetable peeler or a paring knife. Cut the sticks into 2.5 cm (1 inch) pieces and set them aside.

Place the cucumber, lemon juice and Tabasco sauce in a food processor or a blender; process the mixture until it is smooth. Add the celery pieces and purée the mixture. Add the tomatoes and their juice, the salt, sugar, spring onions, ginger and ⅛ teaspoon of the dill seeds, if you are including them, and process the mixture, until it is smooth again.

Chill the mixture for at least 40 minutes. Pour the drink into glasses; sprinkle each serving with a few of the remaining dill seeds if you are using them, then float the reserved celery leaves on top. Insert one or two carrot sticks into each drink and serve.

EDITOR'S NOTE: *To frost the glasses, place them in the freezer for 30 minutes before serving the drink.*

# Chilled Papaya Shake

Makes 4 servings
Working (and total) time: about 15 minutes

Calories **85**
Protein **3g**
Cholesterol **2mg**
Total fat **1g**
Saturated fat **0g**
Sodium **65mg**

| 500 g | ripe papaya, peeled, seeded and cut into chunks | 1 lb |
| 2 tsp | fresh lemon juice | 2 tsp |
| ¼ tsp | ground allspice | ¼ tsp |
| 17.5 cl | fresh orange juice | 6 fl oz |
| 2 tsp | honey | 2 tsp |
| ¼ litre | buttermilk | 8 fl oz |
| 4 | ice cubes | 4 |
| | lemon slices for garnish | |

Put the papaya, lemon juice, ⅛ teaspoon of the allspice, and about half the orange juice into a blender or a food processor, and purée the mixture. Add the honey, buttermilk, the remaining orange juice and the ice, and blend the mixture until it is smooth — about 30 seconds in the blender or 1 minute in the processor.

To serve the papaya shake, pour it into glasses and sprinkle the drinks with some of the remaining allspice. Garnish each shake with a slice of lemon.

# Hot and Spicy Tomato Juice

Makes 4 servings
Working time: about 10 minutes
Total time: about 20 minutes

Calories **40**
Protein **2g**
Cholesterol **0mg**
Total fat **0g**
Saturated fat **0g**
Sodium **18mg**

| 800 g | canned whole tomatoes, puréed in a food processor or a blender and sieved | 1¾ lb |
| 3 tbsp | fresh lime juice | 3 tbsp |
| ⅛ tsp | ground cayenne pepper | ⅛ tsp |
| 2 tbsp | chopped fresh mint | 2 tbsp |
| 4 | lime slices, for garnish (optional) | 4 |

Combine the puréed tomatoes, lime juice, cayenne pepper and mint in a non-reactive saucepan. Heat the mixture over low heat and simmer it for 10 minutes. Garnish each serving with a slice of lime, if you like, and serve the drink hot.

# Raspberry Frappé

Makes 6 servings
Working time: about 20 minutes
Total time: about 1 hour and 45 minutes
(includes chilling)

Calories **130**
Protein **3g**
Cholesterol **4mg**
Total fat **1g**
Saturated fat **1g**
Sodium **30mg**

| | | |
|---|---|---|
| ¾ litre | fresh orange juice | 1 ¼ pints |
| 2 tbsp | instant tapioca | 2 tbsp |
| 2 tbsp | sugar, if you are using fresh raspberries | 2 tbsp |
| 250 g | fresh or frozen raspberries | 8 oz |
| 30 cl | semi-skimmed milk | ½ pint |

Put the orange juice into a non-reactive saucepan; stir in the tapioca and the sugar, if you are using it, and let the mixture stand for 5 minutes. Bring the liquid to the boil, stirring constantly. Remove the pan from the heat and let the mixture cool completely.

Add the raspberries and purée the mixture, one half at a time, in a blender or a food processor. Strain each batch through a fine sieve. Cover the purée with plastic film and chill it for at least 1 hour, then whisk in the milk. If you like, serve the frappé in chilled glasses.

# Banana-Peach Buttermilk Shake

Makes 2 servings
Working time: about 5 minutes
Total time: about 6 hours (includes freezing)

Calories **150**
Protein **5g**
Cholesterol **5mg**
Total fat **2g**
Saturated fat **1g**
Sodium **130mg**

| | | |
|---|---|---|
| 1 | large banana, sliced | 1 |
| 1 | ripe peach, peeled, halved, stoned and sliced | 1 |
| ¼ litre | buttermilk | 8 fl oz |
| 4 tbsp | fresh orange juice | 4 tbsp |
| 2 | strawberries for garnish (optional) | 2 |

Wrap the banana slices in plastic film and freeze them for at least 6 hours. Wrap and freeze the peach slices at the same time.

When you are ready to prepare the shakes, put the banana and peach slices, the buttermilk and orange juice into a food processor or blender; process the mixture until it is smooth — about 1 minute. Pour the purée into tall glasses. If you like, garnish each glass with a strawberry. Serve the shakes at once.

# Orange, Grapefruit and Honeydew Melon with Port

Serves 8
Working (and total) time: about 40 minutes

| | | | |
|---|---|---|---|
| Calories **120** | 1 | grapefruit, preferably pink | 1 |
| Protein **1g** | 2 | oranges | 2 |
| Cholesterol **0mg** | 12.5 cl | ruby port or Madeira | 4 fl oz |
| Total fat **0g** | 12.5 cl | fresh orange juice | 4 fl oz |
| Saturated fat **0g** | 2 tbsp | light or dark brown sugar | 2 tbsp |
| Sodium **20mg** | 1 | honeydew melon, seeded and peeled, the flesh cut into eight wedges and chilled | 1 |

Peel and segment the grapefruit and the oranges as demonstrated below, reserving the juices. Strain the juices into a small saucepan. Put the fruit in a bowl and refrigerate it while you make the sauce.

Add the port or Madeira, the 12.5 cl (4 fl oz) of orange juice and the sugar to the citrus juices in the saucepan, and bring the mixture to the boil. Reduce the heat to medium and simmer the liquid until it is reduced to about 12.5 cl (4 fl oz) — about 25 minutes. Let the sauce cool, then stir it into the fruit in the bowl.

Meanwhile, cut one wedge of honeydew melon in half crosswise, then into thin slices. Spread the slices in the shape of a fan on a chilled individual serving plate. Repeat the process with the remaining wedges. Spoon the citrus segments and the sauce over the melon fans and serve them at once.

## Segmenting a Citrus Fruit

1 *REMOVING THE ENDS. To obtain segments free of pith and membrane from a citrus fruit (here, a grapefruit), use a sharp, stainless steel knife to slice off both ends of the fruit.*

2 *CUTTING OFF THE PEEL. With the fruit standing on a flat end, slice off the peel in vertical strips, following the fruit's contour. Turn the fruit after each cut and continue to remove strips until peel and pith are entirely removed.*

3 *FREEING THE SEGMENTS. Working over a bowl to catch the juices, hold the grapefruit in one hand and carefully slice between flesh and membranes to free each segment. Let the segments fall into the bowl as you detach them.*

# Grapefruit-Apple Compote

Serves 6
Working time: about 25 minutes
Total time: about 3 hours (includes chilling)

Calories **90**
Protein **1g**
Cholesterol **0mg**
Total fat **0g**
Saturated fat **0g**
Sodium **0mg**

| 3 | grapefruits | 3 |
|---|---|---|
| 60 g | caster sugar | 2 oz |
| 2 | sweet green eating apples | 2 |
| 4 | large plums, halved and stoned | 4 |

Finely grate the rind of one grapefruit. Squeeze and strain the juice. Put the rind, juice and sugar into a wide, shallow saucepan. Heat gently until the sugar dissolves. Meanwhile, using an apple corer, remove the cores from the apples. Slice the apples into rings about 3 mm (⅛ inch) thick. Add the apple rings to the hot grapefruit juice and simmer for about 1 minute, just long enough to soften the fruit slightly. Transfer the apples and juice into a bowl.

Cut the peel and all the white pith from the remaining two grapefruits *(page 25)*. Holding each grapefruit over the bowl containing the apples, segment it, cutting between the connecting tissues.

Slice the plum halves horizontally. Add them to the bowl and mix the fruits very gently together. Cover the bowl and refrigerate for 2 to 3 hours, or overnight.

# Orange Slices
# with Pomegranate Seeds

Serves 6
Working time: about 15 minutes
Total time: about 45 minutes (includes chilling)

Calories **75**
Protein **1g**
Cholesterol **0mg**
Total fat **1g**
Saturated fat **0g**
Sodium **3mg**

| | | |
|---|---|---|
| 3 | oranges | 3 |
| 1½ tbsp | finely chopped crystallized ginger | 1½ tbsp |
| 12.5 cl | fresh orange juice | 4 fl oz |
| 1 tbsp | dark rum | 1 tbsp |
| 2 tbsp | sugar | 2 tbsp |
| ½ tsp | pure vanilla extract | ½ tsp |
| 4 tbsp | fresh pomegranate seeds, or one kiwi fruit, peeled, quartered and thinly sliced | 4 tbsp |

Using a sharp, stainless steel knife, cut off both ends of one of the oranges. Stand the orange on end and cut away vertical strips of the peel and pith (page 25, Steps 1 and 2). Slice the orange into 5 mm (¼ inch) thick rounds. Peel and slice the remaining oranges the same way.

Sprinkle the ginger into the bottom of a 22 cm (9 inch) non-reactive pie plate. Arrange the orange slices in a spiral pattern, overlapping them slightly, and set the pie plate aside.

Combine the orange juice, rum and sugar in a small non-reactive saucepan over medium-high heat and boil the mixture for 5 minutes. Remove the pan from the heat and let the syrup cool slightly, then stir in the vanilla extract. Pour the syrup over the orange slices and chill the fruit thoroughly.

Invert a serving plate over the pie plate, quickly turn both over together, and lift away the pie plate. Sprinkle the orange slices with the pomegranate seeds, or scatter the kiwi fruit over the oranges, and serve at once.

# Sliced Apples on Toast

Serves 6
Working time: about 30 minutes
Total time: about 35 minutes

Calories **190**
Protein **3g**
Cholesterol **10mg**
Total fat **5g**
Saturated fat **3g**
Sodium **120mg**

| 30 g | unsalted butter | 1 oz |
|------|-----------------|------|
| 5 | apples, peeled, halved, cored and thinly sliced | 5 |
| 3 tbsp | fresh lemon juice | 3 tbsp |
| 3 tbsp | maple syrup | 3 tbsp |
| 6 | slices wholemeal bread, toasted | 6 |
| 1 tbsp | sugar | 1 tbsp |

Preheat the oven to 240° C (475° F or Mark 9).

Melt the butter in a large, non-stick frying pan over medium heat. Add the apple slices, lemon juice and maple syrup and cook the mixture until the apples are soft — about 5 minutes.

Drain the cooking liquid from the apples into a bowl and set it aside. Allow the apples to cool slightly. Divide the apples equally among the pieces of toast, overlapping the apple slices slightly. Sprinkle each piece of apple toast with some of the sugar.

Bake the apple toast until the apple slices are hot and the bread is very crisp — about 5 minutes. Dribble some of the reserved cooking liquid over each apple toast and serve hot.

# Cardamom Muffins

Makes 12 muffins
Working time: about 15 minutes
Total time: about 40 minutes

Per muffin:
Calories **195**
Protein **4g**
Cholesterol **6mg**
Total fat **6g**
Saturated fat **2g**
Sodium **145mg**

| | | |
|---|---|---|
| 30 g | shelled walnuts | 1 oz |
| 225 g | plain flour | 7½ oz |
| 150 g | caster sugar | 5 oz |
| ½ tsp | ground cinnamon | ½ tsp |
| ½ tsp | baking powder | ½ tsp |
| ¼ tsp | salt | ¼ tsp |
| 30 g | unsalted butter, cut into pieces and chilled | 1 oz |
| 30 g | unsalted polyunsaturated margarine, cut into pieces and chilled | 1 oz |
| 1 tsp | ground cardamom or allspice | 1 tsp |
| 125 g | wholemeal flour | 4 oz |
| ½ tsp | bicarbonate of soda | ½ tsp |
| 30 cl | buttermilk | ½ pint |
| 1 tsp | pure vanilla extract | 1 tsp |

Preheat the oven to 190°C (375°F or Mark 5). Lightly oil 12 cups of a deep bun tin.

In a small baking tin, toast the walnuts in the oven until they are fragrant and slightly darker — about 10 minutes. Set the toasted nuts aside to cool.

In a bowl, combine the plain flour, sugar, cinnamon, baking powder and salt. Using a pastry blender or two knives, cut in the butter and margarine until the mixture resembles coarse meal. Transfer 4 tablespoons of the mixture to a food processor; add the cardamom and the toasted walnuts and process to fine crumbs; this will be used as a topping for the muffins. Set the topping aside.

Add the wholemeal flour and the bicarbonate of soda to the remaining flour mixture and mix them in well. Pour in the buttermilk and vanilla extract, and stir the ingredients just until they are blended; do not overmix.

Spoon the batter into the cups in the bun tin, filling each one about half full. Sprinkle the muffins with the crumb topping. Bake the muffins until they are well browned and firm to the touch — 20 to 25 minutes.

# Irish Soda Scones with Currants and Caraway Seeds

Makes 24 scones
Working time: about 15 minutes
Total time: about 30 minutes

*Per scone:*
Calories **85**
Protein **2g**
Cholesterol **13mg**
Total fat **2g**
Saturated fat **1g**
Sodium **120mg**

| | | |
|---|---|---|
| 300 g | plain flour | 10 oz |
| 125 g | wholemeal flour | 4 oz |
| 2 tbsp | caster sugar | 2 tbsp |
| 2 tsp | baking powder | 2 tsp |
| 1 tsp | bicarbonate of soda | 1 tsp |
| ¼ tsp | salt | ¼ tsp |
| 30 g | cold unsalted polyunsaturated margarine | 1 oz |
| 15 g | cold unsalted butter | ½ oz |
| 1 tbsp | caraway seeds | 1 tbsp |
| 1 | egg | 1 |
| ¼ litre | buttermilk | 8 fl oz |
| 75 g | currants | 2½ oz |
| 2 tbsp | semi-skimmed milk | 2 tbsp |

Preheat the oven to 180°C (350°F or Mark 4). In a bowl, combine the two flours, the sugar, baking powder, bicarbonate of soda and salt. Using a pastry blender or two knives, cut in the margarine and butter until the mixture resembles coarse meal. In another bowl, whisk the caraway seeds, egg and buttermilk together. Stir the buttermilk mixture and the currants into the flour mixture. (The dough will become too stiff to stir before all the flour is mixed in.)

Turn the dough out on to a lightly floured surface and knead it gently just until the flour is incorporated. Roll or pat the dough so that it is about 2 cm (¾ inch) thick. Cut out rounds with a 5 cm (2 inch) biscuit cutter or the rim of a small glass, and place the scones on an ungreased baking sheet. Gather up the scraps of dough, form them into a ball, and repeat the process. Brush the scones with the milk and cut a cross on the top of each with the tip of a sharp knife or a pair of scissors. Bake the scones until they are golden-brown — about 15 minutes. Serve the scones while they are hot.

# Spicy Sweetcorn Sticks

Makes about 18 sticks or wedges
Working time: about 15 minutes
Total time: about 30 minutes

*Per stick:*
Calories **95**
Protein **3g**
Cholesterol **15mg**
Total fat **2g**
Saturated fat **0g**
Sodium **85mg**

| | | |
|---|---|---|
| 175 g | plain flour | 6 oz |
| 125 g | cornmeal | 4 oz |
| 2 tbsp | caster sugar | 2 tbsp |
| ¼ tsp | cayenne pepper | ¼ tsp |
| 1 tbsp | baking powder | 1 tbsp |
| ¼ litre | semi-skimmed milk | 8 fl oz |
| 1 | egg | 1 |
| 2 tbsp | safflower oil | 2 tbsp |
| 6 tbsp | diced sweet red pepper | 6 tbsp |
| 6 tbsp | diced sweet green pepper | 6 tbsp |
| 90 g | fresh or frozen sweetcorn kernels | 3 oz |

Preheat the oven to 230°C (450°F or Mark 8). Lightly oil a corn-stick tin or a 25 cm (10 inch) stainless steel pie plate; heat in the oven for 10 minutes.

Meanwhile, put the flour, cornmeal, sugar, cayenne pepper and baking powder into a bowl and mix them together. In another bowl, whisk together the milk, egg and oil. Pour the milk mixture into the dry ingredients and stir them just until they are blended. Stir in the red and green peppers and the sweetcorn.

If using a corn-stick tin, spoon the batter into the hot tin, filling each mould about three-quarters full. Reduce the oven temperature to 200°C (400°F or Mark 6) and bake the sticks until a wooden toothpick inserted into the centre comes out clean — 10 to 12 minutes. Keep the sticks warm while you bake the remaining batter. Five minutes before the last sweetcorn sticks have finished baking, return the other sticks to the oven to reheat them. Serve at once.

If using a pie plate, spoon the batter into the plate, reduce the heat to 200°C (400°F or Mark 6) and bake for about 25 minutes; cut into wedges to serve.

# Basic Bagels

Makes 12 bagels
Working time: about 1 hour
Total time: about 1 hour and 30 minutes

*Per bagel:*
Calories **135**
Protein **5g**
Cholesterol **0mg**
Total fat **1g**
Saturated fat **0g**
Sodium **95mg**

| | | |
|---|---|---|
| 15 g | easy-blend dried yeast | ½ oz |
| 4 tbsp | caster sugar | 4 tbsp |
| ½ tsp | salt | ½ tsp |
| 300 g | plain flour | 10 oz |
| 175 g | wholemeal flour | 6 oz |
| 30 g | cornmeal | 1 oz |
| 1 | egg white, beaten with 2 tbsp water | 1 |
| 2 tbsp | caraway seeds, sesame seeds or poppy seeds, or ½ small onion, finely chopped (optional) | 2 tbsp |

In a large bowl, stir together the yeast, 2 tablespoons of the sugar, the salt, the plain flour and 60 g (2 oz) of the wholemeal flour. In a small saucepan, heat 35 cl (12 fl oz) of water just until it is hot to the touch (43°C/ 110°F). Pour the water into the yeast-flour mixture and mix the dough thoroughly with a wooden spoon; the dough will be very soft. Gradually stir in enough of the remaining wholemeal flour to form a stiff dough.

Turn the dough out on to a floured surface and knead it until it is smooth and elastic — about 5 minutes. Transfer the dough to a lightly oiled large bowl and turn the dough over to coat it with the oil. Cover the bowl with a damp towel or plastic film and place it in a warm, draught-free place. Let the dough rise until it has doubled in bulk — 15 to 20 minutes.

Meanwhile, pour 3 litres (5 pints) of water into a large pan, add the remaining 2 tablespoons of sugar and heat the water until it is simmering. Preheat the oven to 230°C (450°F or Mark 8). Lightly butter a baking sheet and then sprinkle it with the cornmeal; set the baking sheet aside. If you plan to top the bagels with the chopped onion, lightly oil a small, non-stick frying pan and sauté the onion until it is lightly browned.

Transfer the risen dough to a floured surface. Knock the dough back and then divide it into 12 pieces. Form each piece into a neat ball, rolling it around between the palms of your hands until it is smooth *(Step 1, below)*. To form rings, poke a floured finger through the centre of each ball and move your finger in a circle to widen the hole until it is about 5 cm (2 inches) in diameter. Place the bagels on the work surface, cover them with a towel or plastic film and let them rise until they are slightly larger — about 5 minutes.

With a slotted spoon, carefully put three or four bagels into the simmering water. Poach them for 30 seconds, turn them over, and poach them for 30 seconds more. Lift out the bagels and set them on a kitchen towel to drain. Repeat the process with the remaining bagels. When all of the bagels have been poached and drained, transfer them to the prepared baking sheet. Brush the bagels with the beaten egg white and, if you like, sprinkle them with some of the caraway, sesame or poppy seeds, or the sautéed onion.

Bake the bagels until they are well browned —about 25 minutes. Transfer them to a rack to cool. If you like, serve them with the savoury vegetable spread and the smoked salmon spread *(recipes, page 51)*.

# Variations

## Rye Bagels

Substitute 350 to 375 g (12 to 13 oz) of strong plain flour and 100 g (3½ oz) of rye flour for the flours in the basic recipe.

Combine the yeast, 2 tablespoons of the sugar, the salt, the rye flour and 250 g (8 oz) of the plain flour in a large bowl. Pour in the hot water, as described, and mix the dough thoroughly. Add enough of the remaining plain flour to form a stiff dough, then proceed with the basic bagel recipe.

## Wholemeal and Oat Bran Bagels

Substitute 425 g (15 oz) of strong plain flour, 30 g (1 oz) of oat bran and 30 to 60 g (1 to 2 oz) of wholemeal flour for the flours in the basic recipe.

Combine the yeast, 2 tablespoons of the sugar, the salt, two thirds of the plain flour and the oat bran in a large bowl. Pour in the hot water, as described, and mix the dough thoroughly. Add the remaining plain flour and enough of the wholemeal flour to make a stiff dough, then proceed with the basic bagel recipe.

## Making Bagels

**1** FORMING A BALL. *After dividing the dough into 12 pieces (recipe, above) take a piece and roll it between your palms until it is smooth and spherical. Roll the other 11 pieces in the same manner.*

**2** MAKING THE HOLE. *Lightly flour a finger and press it into the centre of a dough ball. Press hard enough to puncture the dough and touch the work surface beneath.*

**3** ENLARGING THE OPENING. *Place the index fingers of both hands through the hole, and gently rotate your fingers in a spinning motion to enlarge the opening until it is about 5 cm (2 inches) in diameter. Set the bagel aside and proceed to form and shape the other dough balls.*

# Pear Pizza

Serves 8
Working time: about 45 minutes
Total time: about 1 hour and 45 minutes

Calories **210**
Protein **4g**
Cholesterol **4mg**
Total fat **2g**
Saturated fat **1g**
Sodium **35mg**

| | | |
|---|---|---|
| 240 g | strong plain flour | 8½ oz |
| 100 g | caster sugar | 3½ oz |
| 1 tsp | grated lemon rind | 1 tsp |
| ⅛ tsp | salt | ⅛ tsp |
| 1 tbsp | easy-blend dried yeast | 1 tbsp |
| 15 g | unsalted butter | ½ oz |
| 6 tbsp | currants or raisins, coarsely chopped | 6 tbsp |
| 600 g | pears, quartered, cored, peeled and thinly sliced | 1¼ lb |
| 2 tbsp | fresh lemon juice | 2 tbsp |
| 2 tbsp | cornmeal | 2 tbsp |

In a large bowl, combine 75 g (2½ oz) of the flour, 2 tablespoons of the sugar, the lemon rind, salt and yeast. In a small saucepan, heat 17.5 cl (6 fl oz) of water just until it is hot to the touch (43°C/110°F), then pour it into the yeast-flour mixture, and mix the dough thoroughly with a wooden spoon. Gradually stir in enough of the remaining flour to make a dough that can be formed into a ball.

Transfer the dough to a floured surface and knead it until it is smooth and elastic — 5 to 10 minutes. Put the dough into a large, lightly oiled bowl and turn the dough over to coat it with the oil. Cover the bowl with a damp towel or plastic film. Place the bowl in a warm, draught-free place and let the dough rise until it has doubled in bulk — 30 to 45 minutes.

In the meantime, heat the butter in a large, heavy frying pan over medium-high heat. Add the currants or raisins and the pears, and cook the fruit, stirring frequently, for 5 minutes. Add the lemon juice and all but 1 tablespoon of the remaining sugar; continue cooking the mixture until the pears are soft and the sugar begins to brown — about 5 minutes more.

Preheat the oven to 230°C (450°F or Mark 8). Lightly oil a baking sheet and sprinkle it with the cornmeal. When the dough has risen, return it to the floured surface and knead it for 1 minute. Flatten it into a 25 cm (10 inch) round and transfer it to the baking sheet.

Spread the pear topping over the dough, leaving a 1 cm (½ inch) border of dough all round. Sprinkle the reserved tablespoon of sugar over the pear topping, then bake the pizza until the crust is well browned — about 20 minutes. Remove the pizza from the oven and let it stand for about 5 minutes before slicing it into wedges and serving it.

EDITOR'S NOTE: *This pizza can be stored for up to one day, wrapped in aluminium foil, and then reheated, unwrapped, in a 200°C (400°F or Mark 6) oven for 10 minutes.*

# Apple Sauce and Prune Bread

Serves 12
Working time: about 45 minutes
Total time: about 2 hours and 30 minutes
(includes cooling)

Calories **270**
Protein **3g**
Cholesterol **0mg**
Total fat **6g**
Saturated fat **1g**
Sodium **185mg**

| | | |
|---|---|---|
| 135 g | stoned prunes, halved | 4½ oz |
| 6 | large tart apples, peeled, quartered and cored | 6 |
| 300 g | plain flour | 10 oz |
| 25 g | plus 1 tbsp oat bran | ¾ oz |
| 1 tbsp | unsweetened cocoa powder | 1 tbsp |
| 2 tsp | bicarbonate of soda | 2 tsp |
| ¼ tsp | salt | ¼ tsp |
| 1 tsp | ground cinnamon | 1 tsp |
| ½ tsp | grated nutmeg | ½ tsp |
| ¼ tsp | ground cloves | ¼ tsp |
| 100 g | plus 1 tbsp caster sugar | 3½ oz |
| 175 g | honey | 6 oz |
| 4 tbsp | safflower oil | 4 tbsp |

Put the prunes into a small bowl, pour ¼ litre (8 fl oz) of boiling water over them, and set the bowl aside.

Put the apples into a large, heavy-bottomed saucepan and simmer them over low heat, stirring occasionally, until nearly all of the liquid has evaporated and the apples have cooked down to a smooth, thick paste — about 30 minutes. Set the apple sauce aside.

While the apples are simmering, mix the flour, 25 g (¾ oz) of the oat bran, the cocoa powder, bicarbonate of soda, salt, cinnamon, ¼ teaspoon of the nutmeg and the cloves in a large bowl. In another bowl, combine 100 g (3½ oz) of the sugar, the honey and the oil.

Preheat the oven to 180°C (350°F or Mark 4). Lightly oil a 22 by 12 cm (9 by 5 inch) loaf tin.

Stir the apple sauce into the sugar-honey mixture; add the sweetened apple sauce to the flour mixture and stir well to make a smooth batter. Drain the prunes well, fold them into the batter, and spoon the batter into the prepared tin.

In a small bowl, mix the remaining 1 tablespoon of oat bran, the remaining 1 tablespoon of sugar and the remaining ¼ teaspoon of nutmeg; sprinkle this topping over the batter.

Bake the bread until a skewer inserted into its centre comes out clean — 1 hour to 1 hour and 10 minutes. Remove the bread from the oven and let it stand for 5 minutes. Run a knife blade round the sides of the tin, then invert the tin on to a wire rack, and rap it sharply to unmould the bread. Let the bread stand for 30 minutes before slicing and serving it.

# Cheese Pinwheels

Makes 8 pinwheels
Working time: about 30 minutes
Total time: about 45 minutes

*Per pinwheel:*
Calories **210**
Protein **7g**
Cholesterol **2mg**
Total fat **4g**
Saturated fat **1g**
Sodium **270mg**

| | | |
|---|---|---|
| 225 g | plain flour | 7½ oz |
| 90 g | wholemeal flour | 3 oz |
| 3 tbsp | caster sugar | 3 tbsp |
| 2 tsp | baking powder | 2 tsp |
| ½ tsp | bicarbonate of soda | ½ tsp |
| ⅛ tsp | salt | ⅛ tsp |
| ¼ tsp | ground mace or ground cinnamon | ¼ tsp |
| ¼ litre | plain low-fat yogurt | 8 fl oz |
| 2 tbsp | safflower oil | 2 tbsp |
| 30 g | icing sugar, sifted | 1 oz |
| 2 tsp | semi-skimmed milk | 2 tsp |
| **Cheese and lemon filling** | | |
| 125 g | low-fat cottage cheese | 4 oz |
| 2 tsp | caster sugar | 2 tsp |
| 1 | lemon, grated rind only | 1 |

To make the filling, purée the cottage cheese in a food processor until no trace of curd remains. Add the 2 teaspoons of caster sugar and the lemon rind; process the mixture until the ingredients are blended. (Alternatively, press the cheese through a fine sieve, add the sugar and lemon rind, and stir well.) Set aside.

Preheat the oven to 200°C (400°F or Mark 6); lightly oil a baking sheet. Combine the flours, the 3 tablespoons of caster sugar, the baking powder, bicarbonate of soda, salt and mace or cinnamon in a large bowl. In a smaller bowl, whisk together the yogurt and the oil; stir this mixture into the dry ingredients with a wooden spoon. Turn the dough on to a floured surface and knead it once or twice to fully incorporate the ingredients and make a soft dough.

Divide the dough in half. Roll out one half of the dough as shown on the right and trim it into a 20 cm (8 inch) square, then cut the square into four 10 cm (4 inch) squares. Form a pinwheel, using 1 tablespoon of the cheese filling *(Steps 2 to 4, right)*. With a spatula,

transfer the pinwheel to the baking sheet. Repeat the procedure with the remaining dough.

Bake the pinwheels until they are golden-brown — 10 to 12 minutes. Just before the pastries are done, mix the icing sugar and the milk in a small bowl. Dribble or brush the sugar glaze over the pinwheels as soon as they are removed from the oven. Serve the pinwheels hot.

## Forming Pinwheels

1 *SQUARING THE DOUGH. On a lighly floured work surface, roll out half of the dough into a sheet about 22 cm (9 inches) square. With a sharp, small knife, trim the edges to straighten them, then divide the square into quarters (as shown). Discard the trimmings.*

2 *CUTTING CORNERS. Working with one dough square at a time, use the knife tip to slit each corner diagonally to within 2.5 cm (1 inch) of the centre.*

3 *FILLING THE SQUARE. Place a heaped spoonful of the prepared cheese and lemon filling (recipe, left) on to the centre of the dough square.*

4 *FORMING THE PINWHEEL. With your fingers, lift and fold every other point over the filling. Press the last point down on the others to keep them in place. Repeat the procedures to make the other pinwheels.*

# Fruit-Filled Gems

GEMS ARE MINIATURE MUFFINS; MINI BUN TINS ARE AVAILABLE AT
GOURMET AND PROFESSIONAL KITCHEN EQUIPMENT STORES.

Makes 24 gems
Working time: about 45 minutes
Total time: about 1 hour and 15 minutes

*Per gem:*
Calories **83**
Protein **1g**
Cholesterol **15mg**
Total fat **3g**
Saturated fat **1g**
Sodium **30mg**

| | | |
|---|---|---|
| 1 | cooking apple, peeled, cored and coarsely grated | 1 |
| 75 g | dried apricots, chopped | 2½ oz |
| 12.5 cl | unsweetened apple juice | 4 fl oz |
| 1 | lemon, grated rind and juice | 1 |
| 150 g | caster sugar | 5 oz |
| 175 g | plain flour | 6 oz |
| ¼ tsp | baking powder | ¼ tsp |
| 30 g | unsalted butter | 1 oz |
| 30 g | unsalted polyunsaturated margarine | 1 oz |
| 1 | egg, beaten | 1 |
| 2 tbsp | chopped almonds, toasted | 2 tbsp |

Combine the apple, apricots, apple juice, lemon rind and juice, and 4 tablespoons of the sugar in a non-reactive saucepan and bring the mixture to the boil. Reduce the heat and simmer the mixture until the fruit is soft and most of the juice has evaporated — about 15 minutes. Set the filling aside and let it cool.

Combine the remaining sugar with the flour and baking powder in a bowl. Cut the butter and marga-rine into the dry ingredients with a pastry blender or two knives until the mixture resembles coarse meal. With your fingertips, work the egg into the dough just until the egg is incorporated and the dough begins to hold together. Shape two thirds of the dough into a log about 2.5 cm (1 inch) wide, wrap it in plastic film and chill it for 15 minutes. Shape the remaining dough into a round about 1 cm (½ inch) thick; wrap and chill it.

Preheat the oven to 180°C (350°F or Mark 4).

Cut the dough log into 24 pieces and flatten each one slightly. Press one of the pieces into a 4 cm (1½ inch) cup of a mini bun tin to line it, moulding the dough along the sides to the top of the cup. Use the remaining pieces of dough to make 23 more cups. Be careful not to leave any holes in the pastry or the gems will stick to the tin after they are baked. Spoon the fruit filling into the lined cups and sprinkle some of the almonds into each one of them.

Roll out the remaining dough on a lightly floured surface until it is about 3 mm (⅛ inch) thick and cut 24 rounds the same size as the tops of the gem cups. Cover each fruit gem with a round of pastry, lightly pressing on the edges of the pastry to seal them.

Bake the fruit gems until they are browned — 25 to 30 minutes. Let them cool slightly. To remove the gems, cover the tin with a baking sheet or wire rack, turn both over together, and lift off the tin. Serve the fruit gems warm or at room temperature.

# Spring Onion and Rice Muffins

Makes 12 muffins
Working time: about 20 minutes
Total time: about 45 minutes

Per muffin:
Calories **105**
Protein **3g**
Cholesterol **25mg**
Total fat **3g**
Saturated fat **1g**
Sodium **130mg**

| | | |
|---|---|---|
| 45 g | long-grain rice | 1½ oz |
| 225 g | plain flour | 7½ oz |
| 2 tsp | baking powder | 2 tsp |
| 2 tsp | caster sugar | 2 tsp |
| ¼ tsp | salt | ¼ tsp |
| ¼ tsp | ground white pepper | ¼ tsp |
| 1 | egg | 1 |
| 17.5 cl | semi-skimmed milk | 6 fl oz |
| 2 tbsp | safflower oil | 2 tbsp |
| 2 | spring onions, trimmed and finely chopped | 2 |

Preheat the oven to 220°C (425°F or Mark 7). Lightly oil a muffin or deep bun tin. Bring 15 cl (¼ pint) of water to the boil in a saucepan. Stir in the rice, then reduce the heat to low, and cover tightly. Cook the rice until it is tender and all the liquid has been absorbed — 15 to 20 minutes. Uncover and set aside to cool.

Sift the flour, baking powder, sugar, salt and pepper into a bowl. In another bowl, lightly beat the egg, then whisk in the milk and oil; stir in the cooled rice and the spring onions. Pour the rice mixture into the flour mixture, then stir until the ingredients are just blended.

Spoon the batter into the cups in the tin, filling each no more than two-thirds full. Bake the muffins until lightly browned — 18 to 22 minutes. Remove the muffins from the cups immediately and serve hot.

# Plaited Brioche Loaf

Makes 26 slices
Working time: about 20 minutes with a mixer,
30 minutes by hand
Total time: about 8 hours (includes rising)

Per slice:
Calories **100**
Protein **3g**
Cholesterol **20mg**
Total fat **3g**
Saturated fat **1g**
Sodium **45mg**

| | | |
|---|---|---|
| 500 g | strong plain flour | 1 lb |
| ¼ tsp | salt | ¼ tsp |
| 1⅓ tbsp | caster sugar | 1⅓ tbsp |
| 20 g | fresh yeast, or 15 g (½ oz) dried yeast | ¾ oz |
| 2 | eggs | 2 |
| 3 | egg whites | 3 |
| 60 g | unsalted butter, softened | 2 oz |
| 1 tsp | skimmed milk | 1 tsp |

Sift the flour, salt and 1 tablespoon of the sugar into the bowl of an electric mixer — or directly on to the work surface, if you are making the brioche by hand. Make a well in the centre.

Dissolve the fresh yeast in 4 tablespoons of tepid water, or reconstitute the dried yeast according to the manufacturer's instructions. Lightly whisk the eggs and egg whites together. Pour the yeast and eggs into the flour well. Using a dough hook on the mixer, mix on slow speed for 1 minute, then on medium speed for 2 minutes, or until the dough is no longer sticky. Gradually mix in the butter, a little at a time.

If mixing by hand, pour the yeast liquid and eggs into the flour and mix with your fingertips to make a sticky dough. Then, pulling the dough up from the work surface and slapping it back down again, work the dough until it is no longer sticky, and very elastic. Gradually

work in the butter. Put the dough into a clean, lightly floured, bowl. Cover the bowl with plastic film and refrigerate for at least 5 hours, or overnight, to allow the dough to rise slowly; it should treble in size.

Butter a long loaf tin, about 30 by 11 by 7.5 cm (12 by 4½ by 3 inches). Turn the risen dough on to a floured work surface and knead it until smooth — about 1 minute. Divide it into three equal pieces. Roll each piece into a long strand, a little longer than the loaf tin. Place the three strands side by side on the work surface. Starting in the centre, plait the three strands together, working towards yourself. Turn the dough round and plait the other end.

Place the plait in the tin. Cover the tin loosely with plastic film and allow the dough to rise, at room temperature, to the top of the tin — 1 to 1¼ hours. Preheat the oven to 220°C (425°F or Mark 7).

When the dough has risen, stir the milk and remaining sugar together until the sugar dissolves, then brush this glaze evenly over the top of the loaf. Bake for 10 minutes, then reduce the heat to 190°C (375°F or Mark 5), and continue baking for 25 to 30 minutes, until the loaf is golden-brown and sounds hollow when tapped on the base. Turn the loaf on to a wire rack to cool.

EDITOR'S NOTE: *To make individual brioches, divide the dough into 14 equal pieces after the first rising. Cut a quarter off each piece and shape both large and small pieces into balls. Place the large balls in 9 cm (3½ inch) brioche moulds with the small balls on top. Leave to rise for about 30 minutes. Glaze, then bake for 15 to 20 minutes.*

# Ricotta Muffins with Poppy Seeds

Makes 10 muffins
Working time: about 15 minutes
Total time: about 30 minutes

*Per muffin:*
Calories **210**
Protein **7g**
Cholesterol **10mg**
Total fat **7g**
Saturated fat **2g**
Sodium **190mg**

| | | |
|---|---|---|
| 300 g | plain flour | 10 oz |
| 100 g | caster sugar | 3½ oz |
| 1 tsp | bicarbonate of soda | 1 tsp |
| ¼ tsp | salt | ¼ tsp |
| 4 tbsp | poppy seeds | 4 tbsp |
| 250 g | low-fat ricotta cheese | 8 oz |
| 2 tbsp | safflower oil | 2 tbsp |
| 1 | lemon, grated rind only | 1 |
| 1 tbsp | fresh lemon juice | 1 tbsp |
| 17.5 cl | semi-skimmed milk | 6 fl oz |
| 2 | egg whites | 2 |

Preheat the oven to 200°C (400°F or Mark 6). Lightly oil 10 cups in a muffin tin or deep bun tin.

Sift the flour, sugar, bicarbonate of soda and salt into a bowl; stir in the poppy seeds. In another bowl, combine the ricotta, oil, lemon rind and lemon juice, and then whisk in the milk. Add the ricotta mixture to the flour mixture and stir them just until they are blended; do not overmix.

Beat the egg whites until they form soft peaks. Stir half of the beaten egg whites into the ricotta batter, then fold in the remaining egg whites. Spoon the batter into the cups in the prepared tin, filling each cup no more than two-thirds full, and bake the muffins until they are lightly browned — 12 to 14 minutes. Serve the muffins immediately.

## Filled Wholemeal Monkey Bread

THIS IS A REDUCED-FAT VERSION OF MONKEY BREAD, BALLS OF
SWEET YEAST DOUGH BAKED IN A TUBE CAKE TIN.

Serves 8
Working time: about 30 minutes
Total time: about 2 hours and 30 minutes (includes rising)

Calories **350**
Protein **7g**
Cholesterol **10mg**
Total fat **7g**
Saturated fat **3g**
Sodium **155mg**

| | | |
|---|---|---|
| 300 g | strong plain flour | 10 oz |
| 125 g | wholemeal flour | 4 oz |
| 110 g | caster sugar | 3¾ oz |
| ½ tsp | salt | ½ tsp |
| 1 tbsp | easy-blend dried yeast | 1 tbsp |
| ¼ litre | semi-skimmed milk | 8 fl oz |
| 4 tbsp | seedless raisins | 4 tbsp |
| 4 tbsp | sultanas or chopped dried apricots | 4 tbsp |

| | | |
|---|---|---|
| 4 tbsp | chopped walnuts | 4 tbsp |
| 1 tsp | unsweetened cocoa powder | 1 tsp |
| 4 tbsp | dark brown sugar | 4 tbsp |
| 2 tbsp | honey | 2 tbsp |
| 1½ tsp | ground cinnamon | 1½ tsp |
| 30 g | unsalted butter, melted | 1 oz |

To make the bread dough, mix the plain flour, the
wholemeal flour, 1 tablespoon of the caster sugar, the
salt and the yeast together in a large bowl and make a
well in the centre of the dry ingredients. In a small
saucepan, heat the milk just until it is hot to the touch
(43°C/110°F). Stir the hot liquid into the flour mixture.

Turn the dough out on to a floured surface and
knead the dough until it is smooth and elastic — about
10 minutes. Put it into a large bowl, cover the bowl,

and let the dough rise in a warm place until it has doubled in bulk — about 45 minutes.

For the filling, combine the raisins, sultanas or apricots, walnuts, cocoa powder, brown sugar, honey and ½ teaspoon of the cinnamon in a bowl. In another bowl, combine the remaining caster sugar and the remaining cinnamon. Set the bowls aside.

Knock the dough back and turn it out on to a lightly floured surface. Form the dough into a log shape and cut the dough into 16 pieces. Flatten the pieces into 10 cm (4 inch) rounds.

Put about 2 tablespoons of the filling in the middle of each dough round and form a ball (below). Lightly dip the ball into the melted butter, then roll it in the cinnamon-sugar mixture. Repeat this process with the remaining dough rounds and filling. Arrange the balls in a non-stick or lightly oiled 2 litre (3½ pint) capacity tube cake tin or savarin mould with the pinched edges of the balls towards the inside. Cover the pan and let the dough rise until it has again doubled in bulk — about 30 minutes. Meanwhile, preheat the oven to 190°C (375°F or Mark 5).

Bake the bread until it is browned and sounds hollow when tapped — 35 to 45 minutes. Put a serving plate on top of the pan and turn both over to invert the bread on to the plate. Serve the monkey bread warm.

---

## Preparing Monkey Bread

1 FILLING AND FORMING A BALL. After placing about 2 tablespoons of filling on to the middle of a dough round (recipe, left), gather up the sides of the round with your fingers. Pinch the rim together firmly to seal the filling inside.

2 COATING THE BALL. Dip the ball into the small container of melted butter. Then roll the ball in the prepared cinnamon-sugar mixture until it is completely coated.

3 ARRANGING THE BREAD. Put the ball into a non-stick or lightly oiled 2 litre (3½ pint) tube cake tin, with the pinched edge facing the hole of the tin. Fill, form and place the other balls in the same manner, packing them into the tin side by side. Cover the tin and bake as directed in the recipe.

# Potato-Basil Scones

Makes 16 scones
Working time: about 20 minutes
Total time: about 35 minutes

*Per scone:*
Calories **90**
Protein **2g**
Cholesterol **1mg**
Total fat **4g**
Saturated fat **1g**
Sodium **160mg**

| | | |
|---|---|---|
| 1 | potato (about 250 g/8 oz), peeled and cut into eight pieces | 1 |
| 225 g | plain flour | 7½ oz |
| 1 tbsp | baking powder | 1 tbsp |
| ¼ tsp | salt | ¼ tsp |
| 1 tsp | sugar | 1 tsp |
| ¼ tsp | ground white pepper or freshly ground black pepper | ¼ tsp |
| 75 g | unsalted polyunsaturated margarine, cut into small pieces and chilled | 2½ oz |
| 2 tbsp | chopped fresh basil, or 2 tsp dried basil | 2 tbsp |
| 12.5 cl | semi-skimmed milk | 4 fl oz |

Preheat the oven to 220°C (425°F or Mark 7). Put the potato pieces into a saucepan and add enough water to cover them. Bring the water to the boil, then reduce the heat, and simmer the pieces until they are soft — 10 to 15 minutes.

While the potato is cooking, sift the flour, baking powder, salt, sugar and pepper into a bowl. Using two knives or a pastry blender, cut the margarine into the flour mixture until it resembles coarse meal. Stir in the basil, then set the flour mixture aside.

Drain the potato pieces, then transfer them to a bowl. Mash the potato with a potato masher or a fork; alternatively, work the potato through a sieve. Add the milk, then stir the mixture until it is well blended.

Add the flour mixture to the mashed potato. Stir the mixture with a wooden spoon to form a soft dough that does not stick to the bowl. If the mixture seems too dry, stir in additional milk, ½ teaspoon at a time.

Turn the dough out on to a floured surface and knead it gently just until it is smooth and all the ingredients have been incorporated — about eight times. Roll or pat out the dough so that it is about 1 cm (½ inch) thick and cut out rounds with a 5 cm (2 inch) biscuit cutter or the rim of a small glass. Place the scones on an ungreased baking sheet and bake them until they have puffed slightly and are golden-brown — about 15 minutes. Serve the scones immediately.

# Caramel-Orange-Pecan Sticky Buns

Serves 12
Working time: about 25 minutes
Total time: about 45 minutes

Calories **185**
Protein **3g**
Cholesterol **1mg**
Total fat **4g**
Saturated fat **1g**
Sodium **165mg**

| | | |
|---|---|---|
| 2 tbsp | dark brown sugar | 2 tbsp |
| 225 g | plus 1 tbsp plain flour | 7½ oz |
| ½ tsp | ground cinnamon | ½ tsp |
| 60 g | wholemeal flour | 2 oz |
| 1 tbsp | caster sugar | 1 tbsp |
| 1 tbsp | baking powder | 1 tbsp |
| ¼ tsp | salt | ¼ tsp |
| 17.5 cl | semi-skimmed milk | 6 fl oz |
| 2 tbsp | safflower oil | 2 tbsp |
| 1 | orange, grated rind only | 1 |
| 4 tbsp | raisins | 4 tbsp |
| **Caramel-pecan topping** | | |
| 90 g | dark brown sugar | 3 oz |
| 2 tbsp | fresh orange juice | 2 tbsp |
| 2 tbsp | honey | 2 tbsp |
| 30 g | shelled pecans, chopped | 1 oz |

Preheat the oven to 190°C (375°F or Mark 5).

To make the caramel-pecan topping, combine the 90 g (3 oz) of brown sugar, the orange juice and the honey in a small saucepan. Bring the mixture to the boil, reduce the heat and simmer for 1 minute. Stir in the pecans and then pour the topping into a 25 cm (10 inch) ring mould or a 20 cm (8 inch) cake tin.

Combine the 2 tablespoons of brown sugar, 1 tablespoon of the plain flour and the cinnamon in a small bowl; set the bowl aside.

In a larger bowl, combine the remaining plain flour, the wholemeal flour, caster sugar, baking powder and salt. Add the milk, oil and orange rind; stir the ingredients together just until they are blended; do not overmix. Turn the dough out on to a floured surface and gently knead it just until it is smooth. Roll the dough into a 20 by 30 cm (8 by 12 inch) oblong. Sprinkle the dough evenly with the reserved cinnamon mixture, then with the raisins.

Beginning with a long side, roll the dough into a log. Cut the log into 12 slices. Set the slices in the mould or tin, on top of the pecan mixture. Bake the cake until it is brown and the pecan mixture is bubbly — 20 to 25 minutes. Remove the tin from the oven and invert it immediately on to a large serving platter. Break apart the buns and serve warm.

# Wheat Berry Muffins

Makes 12 muffins
Working time: about 20 minutes
Total time: about 2 hours

Per muffin:
Calories **210**
Protein **7g**
Cholesterol **45mg**
Total fat **4g**
Saturated fat **1g**
Sodium **210mg**

| | | |
|---|---|---|
| 100 g | wheat berries | 3½ oz |
| 175 g | plain flour | 6 oz |
| 125 g | wholemeal flour | 4 oz |
| 60 g | dried skimmed milk | 2 oz |
| 1 tsp | baking powder | 1 tsp |
| 1 tsp | bicarbonate of soda | 1 tsp |
| ½ tsp | ground cinnamon | ½ tsp |
| ¼ tsp | salt | ¼ tsp |
| 2 | eggs | 2 |
| 90 g | honey | 3 oz |
| 2 tbsp | safflower oil | 2 tbsp |
| 35 cl | buttermilk | 12 fl oz |
| 75 g | raisins | 2½ oz |

Bring ¼ litre (8 fl oz) of water to the boil in a saucepan and then add the wheat berries. Reduce the heat to low, cover the pan and simmer the kernels until they are tender — 1½ to 2 hours. If the wheat berries absorb all the water before they finish cooking, pour in more water, 4 tablespoons at a time, to keep them from burning. Drain them and set them aside.

Preheat the oven to 190°C (375°F or Mark 5). Lightly oil 12 cups in a muffin tin or deep bun tin. Stir together the two flours, the dried milk, baking powder, bicarbonate of soda, cinnamon and salt in a bowl. In another bowl, mix the eggs with the honey and the oil and stir in the buttermilk. Combine the egg mixture with the flour mixture and stir just until they are blended; do not overmix. Fold in the wheat berries and raisins.

Spoon the batter into the cups in the tin, filling each one no more than two-thirds full. Bake the muffins until they are golden-brown — 16 to 18 minutes. Serve the muffins immediately.

# Wheat Berry Bread

Makes 3 loaves
Working time: about 45 minutes
Total time: about 4 hours (includes rising)

*Per slice:*
Calories **105**
Protein **4g**
Cholesterol **6mg**
Total fat **1g**
Saturated fat **0g**
Sodium **40mg**

| | | |
|---|---|---|
| 200 g | wheat berries | 7½ oz |
| 1 tbsp | easy-blend dried yeast | 1 tbsp |
| 2 tsp | caster sugar | 2 tsp |
| 4 tbsp | dried skimmed milk | 4 tbsp |
| 90 g | honey | 3 oz |
| 90 g | molasses | 3 oz |
| 45 g | wheat germ | 1½ oz |
| ¼ tsp | salt | ¼ tsp |
| 1 to 1.2 kg | strong plain flour | 2 to 2½ lb |
| 1 | egg, beaten | 1 |
| ½ tsp | coarse salt | ½ tsp |

Put the wheat berries and ¾ litre (1¼ pints) of water into a saucepan and bring the water to the boil. Reduce the heat and simmer the wheat berries until they are tender — 1½ to 2 hours. Let the wheat berries cool in the cooking liquid, then drain them over a bowl; reserve the liquid.

Combine the yeast, sugar, dried milk, honey, molasses, wheat germ, salt and drained wheat berries with 825 g (30 oz) of the flour in a large bowl. Measure the reserved cooking liquid and add enough water to make ¾ litre (1¼ pints) of liquid. Heat the liquid just until it is hot to the touch (43°C/110°F). Pour the hot liquid into the flour mixture and stir them together with a wooden spoon.

Gradually incorporate as much of the remaining flour as needed, working it in with your hands until the dough becomes stiff but not dry. Turn the dough out on to a floured surface and knead the dough until it is smooth and elastic — 5 to 10 minutes. Place the dough in a clean, oiled bowl; turn the dough over to coat it with the oil, cover the bowl with a damp towel or plastic film, and let the dough rise in a warm, draught-free place until it is doubled in size — about 45 minutes.

Knock the dough back and divide it into three pieces. Knead one piece of the dough and form it into a ball. Knead and form the remaining two pieces of dough into balls. Put the balls of dough on to a large baking sheet, leaving enough space between the loaves for them to expand. Cover the loaves and let them rise until they are doubled in volume again — about 30 minutes.

About 10 minutes before the end of the rising time, preheat the oven to 180°C (350°F or Mark 4).

Bake the loaves for 25 minutes. Remove the baking sheet from the oven, brush each loaf with some of the beaten egg, then sprinkle each with a little of the coarse salt. Return the loaves to the oven and continue to bake them until they are brown and sound hollow when tapped on the bottom — 25 to 30 minutes. Cool to room temperature; each loaf yields 16 slices.

EDITOR'S NOTE: *If you plan to store the bread, it is preferable to keep it in the freezer. Refrigeration causes bread to dry out.*

## Pear Butter

Makes 35 cl (12 fl oz)
Working time: about 25 minutes
Total time: about 2 hours

Per tablespoon:
Calories **30**
Protein **0g**
Cholesterol **0mg**
Total fat **0g**
Saturated fat **0g**
Sodium **1mg**

| 1 kg | ripe pears, peeled, quartered, cored and cut into 2.5 cm (1 inch) pieces | 2 lb |
|---|---|---|
| ¼ litre | unsweetened apple juice | 8 fl oz |
| 1 tbsp | light or dark brown sugar | 1 tbsp |
| ¼ tsp | ground allspice | ¼ tsp |
| ⅛ tsp | ground cinnamon | ⅛ tsp |
| 1½ tbsp | pear liqueur or brandy | 1½ tbsp |

Combine the pears, unsweetened apple juice, brown sugar, allspice and cinnamon in a large, heavy-bottomed saucepan. Bring the mixture to a simmer over medium heat, then reduce the heat to maintain a slow simmer. Continue to cook the pears, stirring occasionally, until they are very soft and all the liquid has evaporated — about 1½ hours.

Put the pear mixture into a blender or a food processor, and add the liqueur or brandy. Process the mixture until the pears are smoothly puréed. Spoon the pear butter into a serving bowl and leave it to cool. Serve it at room temperature. Pear butter can be made up to a week in advance; cover it and store it in the refrigerator.

## Apricot Spread

Makes 35 cl (12 fl oz)
Working time: about 10 minutes
Total time: about 25 minutes

Per tablespoon:
Calories **29**
Protein **0g**
Cholesterol **0mg**
Total fat **0g**
Saturated fat **0g**
Sodium **1mg**

| 250 g | dried apricots | 8 oz |
|---|---|---|
| 35 cl | unsweetened apple juice | 12 fl oz |
| ⅛ tsp | ground allspice | ⅛ tsp |
| ½ tsp | ground cumin | ½ tsp |

Put the apricots, apple juice, allspice and cumin into a non-reactive saucepan. Bring the mixture to a simmer and cook it, stirring occasionally, until only about 12.5 cl (4 fl oz) of liquid remains — 10 to 15 minutes. Purée the mixture in a food processor for 5 seconds, then scrape down the sides, and process again to make a thick, chunky spread — about 10 seconds. The spread may be kept refrigerated for up to two weeks.

# Apple-Rhubarb Butter

Makes 1 litre (1¾ pints)
Working (and total) time: about 45 minutes

| Per tablespoon: | | | |
| --- | --- | --- | --- |
| Calories **12** | 500 g | fresh rhubarb, cut into 2.5 cm (1 inch) pieces, or frozen rhubarb, thawed | 1 lb |
| Protein **0g** | | | |
| Cholesterol **0mg** | 350 g | tart apples, peeled, cored and sliced | 12 oz |
| Total fat **0g** | 1 | orange, grated rind and juice | 1 |
| Saturated fat **0g** | 100 g | sugar | 3½ oz |
| Sodium **0mg** | ¼ tsp | ground mace or grated nutmeg | ¼ tsp |

Put the rhubarb, apples, orange rind, orange juice and sugar into a heavy-bottomed saucepan. Cook the mixture over medium-low heat, stirring occasionally with a wooden spoon to break up the pieces of fruit, until the mixture is very thick — 25 to 30 minutes. Stir in the mace or nutmeg, and serve the apple-rhubarb butter warm with griddle cakes or French toast, or chilled with muffins or scones.

# Fresh Yogurt Cheese

Makes about 300 g (10 oz)
Working time: about 20 minutes
Total time: about 8 hours

| Per tablespoon: | | |
| --- | --- | --- |
| Calories **18** | ¾ litre | plain low-fat yogurt | 1¼ pints |
| Protein **0g** | | | |
| Cholesterol **2mg** | | | |
| Total fat **0g** | | | |
| Saturated fat **0g** | | | |
| Sodium **10mg** | | | |

Line a large sieve with a double layer of muslin or a large, round paper coffee filter. Place the lined sieve over a deep bowl so that the yogurt can effectively drain; spoon the yogurt into the sieve. Cover the bowl and sieve with plastic film. Put the bowl in the refrigerator and let the yogurt drain overnight.

Discard the whey that has collected in the bowl and transfer the yogurt cheese to another bowl; the cheese should be very thick. Cover the bowl with plastic film and refrigerate the cheese until you are ready to use it. Yogurt cheese will keep in the refrigerator for two weeks.

## Transforming Yogurt into Tangy Cheese Spreads

Yogurt plays an important role in a healthy, low-fat diet. In cooking, it provides a tasty alternative to soured cream and double cream. And with the simple cheese making technique presented on the left, yogurt can even take the place of cream cheese in your breakfast or brunch menu, especially when it is combined with other ingredients to produce savoury spreads.

Yogurt cheese made from plain low-fat yogurt has all the delectability of full-fat soft cheese or cream cheese, but has up to 75 per cent less calories and only about 2 per cent saturated fat. Its lighter texture (yogurt cheese contains no gum arabic, a thickener often found in commercial soft cheeses) and its tart, fresh flavour recommend it for morning meals and snacks. Furthermore, yogurt cheese is easily digested and can be readily eaten by many who have lactose intolerance.

# Dill and Chive Spread

Makes about 300 g (10 oz)
Working (and total) time: about 15 minutes

Per tablespoon:
Calories **20**
Protein **2g**
Cholesterol **2mg**
Total fat **0g**
Saturated fat **0g**
Sodium **30mg**

| | | |
|---|---|---|
| 300 g | yogurt cheese (recipe, opposite page) | 10 oz |
| 2 tbsp | finely cut fresh dill | 2 tbsp |
| 2 tbsp | finely cut fresh chives | 2 tbsp |
| ¼ tsp | salt | ¼ tsp |
| | freshly ground black pepper | |

Combine the yogurt cheese with the dill, chives, salt and a generous grinding of pepper. The spread may be served at once or covered and refrigerated until you are ready to use it.

# Savoury Vegetable Spread

Makes about 350 g (12 oz)
Working time: about 30 minutes
Total time: about 2 hours and 30 minutes
(includes chilling)

Per tablespoon:
Calories **15**
Protein **1g**
Cholesterol **1mg**
Total fat **0g**
Saturated fat **0g**
Sodium **40mg**

| | | |
|---|---|---|
| 1 | small carrot, finely shredded or grated | 1 |
| 1 | small sweet red pepper, seeded, deribbed and quartered, the flesh finely grated and the skin discarded | 1 |
| 3 | radishes, finely grated | 3 |
| ½ | small onion, finely grated | ½ |
| ½ tsp | salt | ½ tsp |
| 2 | garlic cloves, finely chopped | 2 |
| 2 tsp | fresh thyme, finely chopped, or ½ tsp dried thyme leaves | 2 tsp |
| 300 g | yogurt cheese (recipe, opposite page) | 10 oz |

Put the carrot and red pepper into a small, non-stick frying pan and cook them over low heat until most of their moisture has evaporated — 3 to 4 minutes. Let the vegetables cool.

Stir the cooled carrot and red pepper, along with the radishes, onion, salt, garlic and thyme, into the yogurt cheese. So that the flavours can meld, refrigerate the spread for at least 2 hours before serving it.

# Smoked Salmon Spread

Makes about 350 g (12 oz)
Working time: about 15 minutes
Total time: about 2 hours and 15 minutes
(includes chilling)

Per tablespoon:
Calories **20**
Protein **2g**
Cholesterol **3mg**
Total fat **1g**
Saturated fat **0g**
Sodium **20mg**

| | | |
|---|---|---|
| 300 g | yogurt cheese (recipe, opposite page) | 10 oz |
| 3 tbsp | finely cut fresh chives or spring onions | 3 tbsp |
| 45 g | smoked salmon, very finely chopped | 1½ oz |
| ¼ tsp | white pepper | ¼ tsp |
| ⅛ tsp | paprika, preferably Hungarian | ⅛ tsp |
| 1 tsp | fresh lemon juice | 1 tsp |
| ⅛ tsp | salt | ⅛ tsp |

Combine the yogurt cheese with the chives, salmon, pepper, paprika, lemon juice and salt. So that the flavours can meld, refrigerate the spread for at least 2 hours before serving it.

# Sage and Black Pepper Waffles with Spiced Apple Sauce

Makes six 18 cm (7 inch) round waffles
Working (and total) time: about 45 minutes

*Per waffle:*
Calories **445**
Protein **10g**
Cholesterol **45mg**
Total fat **11g**
Saturated fat **1g**
Sodium **305mg**

| | | |
|---|---|---|
| 300 g | plain flour | 10 oz |
| 2 tsp | baking powder | 2 tsp |
| 2 tbsp | caster sugar | 2 tbsp |
| 2 tbsp | chopped fresh sage, or 2 tsp dried sage | 2 tbsp |
| 60 g | cornmeal | 2 oz |
| ¼ tsp | salt | ¼ tsp |
| ¾ tsp | freshly ground black pepper | ¾ tsp |
| 1 | egg, separated, plus 2 egg whites | 1 |
| ½ litre | skimmed milk | 16 fl oz |
| 4 tbsp | safflower oil | 4 tbsp |
| **Spiced apple sauce** | | |
| 750 g | tart apples, peeled, cored and cut into chunks | 1½ lb |
| 4 tbsp | sugar | 4 tbsp |
| 4 tbsp | unsweetened apple juice or water | 4 tbsp |
| ¼ tsp | grated nutmeg | ¼ tsp |

To make the spiced apple sauce, first put the apples, the sugar and the juice or water into a heavy-bottomed non-reactive saucepan. Bring the mixture to the boil. Reduce the heat and simmer the mixture, stirring occasionally, until the apples begin to loose their shape —

20 to 25 minutes. Remove the pan from the heat and stir in the nutmeg; the apple sauce will be chunky. Cover the pan and set the apple sauce aside while you make the waffles.

Sift the flour, baking powder and sugar into a bowl; stir in the sage, cornmeal, salt and pepper. In a second bowl, beat the egg yolk lightly and then whisk in the milk and oil. In another bowl, beat the egg whites until they form soft peaks. Make a well in the centre of the flour mixture and pour in the milk mixture. Stir the batter just until it is blended; some lumps will remain. Stir about a quarter of the egg whites into the batter, then gently fold in the remaining whites.

Prepare the waffle iron according to the manufacturer's instructions. Ladle enough of the batter on to the preheated surface of the grid to cover it by about two thirds. Close the lid and bake the waffle until steam no longer escapes from the sides of the iron and the waffle is crisp and golden — 3 to 5 minutes. Serve the waffle immediately, topped with some of the apple sauce; if the apple sauce has cooled, reheat it beforehand. Continue making waffles in the same manner until no batter remains. Although these waffles are best served immediately, you may transfer them as you make them to an ovenproof plate and keep them in a 100°C (200°F or Mark ¼) oven until all are ready.

EDITOR'S NOTE: *The spiced apple sauce for this recipe can be prepared up to one day ahead, stored in the refrigerator, and heated just before serving.*

# Gingerbread Waffles

Serves 6
Working (and total) time: about 30 minutes

Calories **355**
Protein **11g**
Cholesterol **50mg**
Total fat **7g**
Saturated fat **1g**
Sodium **315mg**

| | | |
|---|---|---|
| 150 g | plain flour | 5 oz |
| 125 g | wholemeal flour | 4 oz |
| 100 g | caster sugar | 3½ oz |
| 1 tsp | ground cinnamon | 1 tsp |
| 1 tsp | ground ginger | 1 tsp |
| 1 tsp | dry mustard | 1 tsp |
| ½ tsp | bicarbonate of soda | ½ tsp |
| ½ tsp | baking powder | ½ tsp |
| ¼ tsp | ground cloves | ¼ tsp |
| ¼ tsp | salt | ¼ tsp |
| 30 cl | buttermilk | ½ pint |
| 1 | egg, separated, plus 1 egg white | 1 |
| 90 g | dark molasses | 3 oz |
| 2 tbsp | safflower oil | 2 tbsp |
| 1 | lemon, rind only, julienned | 1 |

**Lemon-yogurt topping**

| | | |
|---|---|---|
| ¼ litre | plain low-fat yogurt | 8 fl oz |
| 1 tbsp | fresh lemon juice | 1 tbsp |
| 1 | egg white | 1 |
| 2 tbsp | caster sugar | 2 tbsp |

To make the topping, combine the yogurt and lemon juice in a bowl. Beat the egg white with the sugar in another bowl until soft peaks form. Fold the beaten egg white into the yogurt mixture. Set the topping aside while you make the waffles.

Combine the flours, sugar, cinnamon, ginger, mustard, bicarbonate of soda, baking powder, cloves and salt in a bowl. In another bowl, whisk together the buttermilk, egg yolk, molasses and oil; pour this mixture into the dry ingredients. Stir the batter until the ingredients are just blended; do not overmix.

Beat the two egg whites until they form soft peaks. Gently fold them into the batter. Prepare the waffle iron according to the manufacturer's instructions. Ladle enough of the batter on to the preheated surface of the grid to cover it by two thirds. Close the lid and bake the waffle until steam no longer escapes from the sides of the iron and the waffle is crisp and golden — 3 to 5 minutes. Continue making waffles in the same manner until all of the batter is used. Although these waffles are best served immediately, you may transfer them to an ovenproof plate as you make them, and keep them warm in a 100°C (200°F or Mark ¼) oven until all are ready.

Garnish the waffles with some of the lemon rind and serve them with the lemon-yogurt topping.

# Overnight French Toast

ALLOWING THE SOAKED BREAD SLICES TO REST OVERNIGHT
YIELDS SOFT AND CREAMY CENTRES.

Serves 6
Working time: about 30 minutes
Total time: about 8 hours and 30 minutes
(includes chilling)

Calories **300**
Protein **12g**
Cholesterol **100mg**
Total fat **4g**
Saturated fat **2g**
Sodium **530mg**

| | | |
|---|---|---|
| 1 | loaf (about 500 g/1 lb) French bread, the ends trimmed | 1 |
| 2 | eggs, plus 2 egg whites | 2 |
| 6 tbsp | caster sugar | 6 tbsp |
| 2 | lemons, grated rind only | 2 |
| ¼ tsp | salt | ¼ tsp |
| ½ litre | semi-skimmed milk | 16 fl oz |
| 2 tbsp | light or dark rum, or 1 tsp pure vanilla extract | 2 tbsp |
| | freshly grated nutmeg | |

Cut the bread into 12 slices about 2 cm (¾ inch) thick. In a large, shallow dish, whisk together the eggs, egg whites, sugar, lemon rind and salt, then whisk in the milk and the rum or vanilla extract.

Dip the bread slices into the egg-and-milk mixture, turning them once or twice until they are thoroughly soaked with the liquid. Transfer the slices to a large plate as you work. Dribble any liquid remaining in the dish over the slices, then sprinkle some nutmeg over them. Cover the slices with plastic film and refrigerate them overnight.

Preheat the oven to 200°C (400°F or Mark 6). Heat a large griddle or frying pan (box, opposite page) over medium heat until a few drops of cold water dance when sprinkled on the surface. Put as many prepared bread slices as will fit on the griddle or pan and cook them until the undersides are golden — about 3 minutes. Turn the slices and cook them until the second sides are lightly browned — 2 to 3 minutes more. Transfer the slices to a baking sheet. Brown the remaining slices and transfer them to the baking sheet.

Place the baking sheet in the oven and bake the French toast until it is cooked through and has puffed up — about 10 minutes. Serve it hot with blueberry syrup (opposite page) or another topping of your choice.

# Blueberry Syrup

Makes about 90 cl (1½ pints)
Working (and total) time: about 15 minutes

| Per 3 tablespoons: | | | |
|---|---|---|---|
| Calories **55** | 300 g | fresh blueberries or blackcurrants, picked over and stemmed, or frozen blueberries or blackcurrants | 10 oz |
| Protein **0g** | | | |
| Cholesterol **0mg** | | | |
| Total fat **0g** | 200 g | sugar | 7 oz |
| Saturated fat **0g** | 1 | lemon, rind julienned and juice reserved | 1 |
| Sodium **1mg** | 1 | orange, rind julienned and juice reserved | 1 |

| | | |
|---|---|---|
| 1 tbsp | cornflour, mixed with 1 tbsp water | 1 tbsp |

Combine ¼ litre (8 fl oz) of water, the blueberries or blackcurrants, sugar, lemon rind and lemon juice, and orange rind and orange juice in a saucepan; bring the mixture to the boil. Reduce the heat to medium low and simmer the berries, stirring, for 1 minute.

Remove the saucepan from the heat and stir in the cornflour mixture. Return the pan to the heat and simmer the syrup until it becomes thick and clear — about 1 minute more.

## Oiling Griddles and Frying Pans

While the higher fat content of traditional recipes allows you to cook on the well-seasoned surface of a griddle or frying pan without using additional fat, the low-fat recipes in this book often require a slightly different approach to guard against sticking.

A non-stick griddle or frying pan that has been maintained according to the manufacturer's instructions need not be oiled. However, if either is beginning to show signs of wear — particularly scratches — it is a good idea to coat the surface with a film of oil. Pour ¼ teaspoon of safflower oil on to the griddle or into the frying pan and rub it all over the bottom with a paper towel. Do not discard the towel; it will have absorbed enough oil to allow you to coat the surface several times as needed during the cooking process.

A well-seasoned, heavy griddle or frying pan that does not have a non-stick surface should be treated in the same way, but with 1 teaspoon of oil instead of ¼ teaspoon. In both cases, most of the oil will be retained by the towel and thus have little effect on the final calorie count

# Wholemeal Yogurt Waffles with Fruit

Makes about six 18 cm (7 inch) round waffles
Working (and total) time: about 30 minutes

*Per waffle:*
Calories **395**
Protein **16g**
Cholesterol **95mg**
Total fat **11g**
Saturated fat **2g**
Sodium **395mg**

| | | |
|---|---|---|
| 350 g | fresh strawberries, hulled and quartered | 12 oz |
| 150 g | diced ripe papaya (or mango, peach, melon or pineapple) | 5 oz |
| 2 tbsp | honey | 2 tbsp |
| 150 g | plain flour | 5 oz |
| 125 g | wholemeal flour | 4 oz |
| 100 g | wheat germ | 3½ oz |
| 1 tsp | baking powder | 1 tsp |
| ½ tsp | bicarbonate of soda | ½ tsp |
| ½ tsp | salt | ½ tsp |
| 2 | eggs, separated | 2 |
| 2 tbsp | safflower oil | 2 tbsp |
| 3 tbsp | light or dark brown sugar | 3 tbsp |
| ¼ litre | semi-skimmed milk | 8 fl oz |
| ¼ litre | plain low-fat yogurt | 8 fl oz |

Combine the fruit with the honey and let the mixture stand at room temperature for 30 minutes.

Put the two flours, the wheat germ, baking powder, bicarbonate of soda and salt into a bowl. In another bowl, lightly beat the egg yolks with the oil and brown sugar. Stir in the milk and yogurt. Pour the yogurt mixture into the flour mixture. Stir the ingredients together until they are just blended; do not overmix the batter.

Prepare the waffle iron according to the manufacturer's instructions. Beat the egg whites until they form soft peaks and then fold them into the batter. Ladle enough of the batter on to the preheated surface of the grid to cover it by about two thirds. Close the lid and bake the waffle until steam no longer escapes from the sides of the iron and the waffle is crisp and golden — 3 to 5 minutes. Serve the waffle at once, topped with the fruit, and continue making waffles in the same manner until all of the batter is used. Although these waffles are best served immediately, you may transfer them as you make them to an oven-proof plate and keep them in a 100°C (200°F or Mark ¼) oven until all are ready.

# Apple French Toast

Serves 6
Working (and total) time: about 30 minutes

Calories **315**
Protein **10g**
Cholesterol **95mg**
Total fat **5g**
Saturated fat **2g**
Sodium **455mg**

| | | |
|---|---|---|
| 1 | loaf (about 500 g/1 lb) unsliced day-old dense white bread, crusts removed | 1 |
| 2 | eggs, plus 2 egg whites | 2 |
| 2 tbsp | caster sugar | 2 tbsp |
| ¼ tsp | salt | ¼ tsp |
| ¼ litre | semi-skimmed milk | 8 fl oz |
| 12.5 cl | unsweetened apple juice | 4 fl oz |
| 1 | orange (optional), peeled and thinly sliced, slices halved | 1 |

**Apple compote**

| | | |
|---|---|---|
| 1 | apple, preferably Granny Smith, peeled, quartered, cored and chopped | 1 |
| ¼ litre | unsweetened apple juice | 8 fl oz |
| 12.5 cl | fresh orange juice | 4 fl oz |
| 6 tbsp | sugar | 6 tbsp |
| 2 tbsp | currants | 2 tbsp |
| 1 | orange, grated rind only | 1 |
| ¼ tsp | grated nutmeg | ¼ tsp |
| | pinch of salt | |
| 1 tbsp | cornflour, mixed with 1 tbsp water | 1 tbsp |

Cut the bread into 12 slices about 1 cm (½ inch) thick; cut each slice into four strips. In a large, shallow dish, whisk together the eggs, egg whites, sugar and salt, then whisk in the milk and the apple juice.

Dip the bread strips into the egg-and-milk mixture, turning them once or twice until they are thoroughly soaked with the liquid. Transfer the strips to a large plate or baking sheet as you work. Dribble any liquid left in the dish over the strips.

To make the apple compote, combine the chopped apple, the apple juice, orange juice, sugar, currants, orange rind, nutmeg and salt in a saucepan. Bring the liquid to the boil, reduce the heat to medium low and simmer the compote until the apple is barely tender — about 5 minutes. Remove the pan from the heat and stir in the cornflour mixture. Return the pan to the heat and simmer the compote, stirring, until it is thick and clear — about 1 minute. Transfer the compote to a serving bowl and keep it warm.

Heat a large griddle or frying pan *(box, page 55)* over medium heat until a few drops of cold water dance when sprinkled on the surface. Cook the prepared strips of bread until the undersides are golden —about 3 minutes. Turn the strips over and cook them until the second sides are lightly browned — 2 to 3 minutes more. Transfer the French toast strips to a platter and keep them warm while you cook the remaining strips.

Serve the French toast at once, garnished with the orange slices, if you are using them, and accompanied by the apple compote.

## Spicy Shrimp Griddle Cakes

Serves 6
Working (and total) time: about 30 minutes

Calories **245**
Protein **12g**
Cholesterol **70mg**
Total fat **6g**
Saturated fat **3g**
Sodium **295mg**

| Metric | Ingredient | Imperial |
|---|---|---|
| 150 g | cornmeal | 5 oz |
| 75 g | plain flour | 2½ oz |
| 2 tsp | baking powder | 2 tsp |
| 1 tsp | dried thyme | 1 tsp |
| 1 tsp | dried oregano | 1 tsp |
| ¼ tsp | salt | ¼ tsp |
| ¼ tsp | ground white pepper | ¼ tsp |
| ¼ tsp | cayenne pepper | ¼ tsp |
| 3 | large garlic cloves, finely chopped | 3 |
| 1 | spring onion, finely chopped | 1 |
| 1 | small sweet red pepper, seeded, deribbed and finely chopped | 1 |
| 30 g | unsalted butter, melted | 1 oz |
| 40 cl | semi-skimmed milk | 13 fl oz |
| 250 g | cooked, peeled shrimps | 8 oz |
| 1 | lemon, cut into wedges, for garnish | 1 |
| | several parsley sprigs for garnish | |

Combine the cornmeal, flour, baking powder, thyme, oregano, salt, white pepper and cayenne pepper in a bowl. Stir in the garlic, spring onion and red pepper. Whisk in the melted butter and the milk, mixing until all the ingredients are just blended. Stir in the shrimps.

Heat a large griddle or frying pan (box, page 55) over medium heat until a few drops of cold water dance when sprinkled on the surface. Drop the batter a generous tablespoon at a time on to the griddle and use the back of the spoon to spread the batter into rounds. Cook the griddle cakes until they are covered with bubbles and the undersides are golden — 1 to 3 minutes. Flip the griddle cakes and cook them until the second sides are lightly browned — about 1 minute more. Transfer the griddle cakes to a platter and keep them warm while you cook the remaining batter. Serve the griddle cakes piping hot, garnished with the lemon wedges and parsley sprigs.

# Tropical Puffed Pancake

Serves 4
Working time: about 30 minutes
Total time: about 45 minutes

Calories **350**
Protein **9g**
Cholesterol **140mg**
Total fat **8g**
Saturated fat **2g**
Sodium **265mg**

| | | |
|---|---|---|
| 3 tbsp | caster sugar | 3 tbsp |
| ¼ tsp | ground cinnamon | ¼ tsp |
| 35 g | plain flour | 1¼ oz |
| 30 g | wholemeal flour | 1 oz |
| ½ tsp | baking powder | ½ tsp |
| ¼ tsp | salt | ¼ tsp |
| 2 | eggs, separated, plus 1 egg white | 2 |
| 1 tbsp | light or dark rum | 1 tbsp |
| 1 tbsp | safflower oil | 1 tbsp |
| 1 | lemon, grated rind only | 1 |
| 17.5 cl | semi-skimmed milk | 6 fl oz |
| 2 | bananas, sliced diagonally into 5 mm (¼ inch) thick ovals | 2 |
| **Rum-pineapple topping** | | |
| 300 g | fresh pineapple flesh, coarsely chopped, or canned unsweetened pineapple chunks, drained and coarsely chopped | 10 oz |
| 2 tbsp | dark brown sugar | 2 tbsp |
| 2 tbsp | raisins | 2 tbsp |
| 1 | lemon, juice only | 1 |
| 2 tbsp | light or dark rum | 2 tbsp |

To make the rum-pineapple topping, put the pineapple into a heavy-bottomed saucepan and stir in the brown sugar, raisins and lemon juice. Bring the mixture to the boil, then reduce the heat, and simmer the mixture for 5 minutes. Remove the pan from the heat and stir in the rum. Keep the topping warm while you prepare the puffed pancake.

In a small bowl, mix 2 tablespoons of the caster sugar with the cinnamon; set the cinnamon sugar aside. Preheat the oven to 220°C (425°F or Mark 7).

Sift the two flours, the baking powder, the salt and the remaining caster sugar into a bowl. In a separate bowl, whisk the egg yolks with the rum and the oil; stir in the lemon rind and the milk. Whisk the flour mixture into the milk mixture to make a smooth, thin batter.

Beat the egg whites until they form soft peaks. Stir half of the egg whites into the batter and then fold in the remaining egg whites.

Heat a 30 cm (12 inch) shallow fireproof casserole over medium heat. Ladle the batter into the casserole. Cook the pancake for 2 minutes; top it with the sliced bananas and sprinkle it with the cinnamon sugar. Put the casserole into the oven and bake the pancake until it puffs up and is golden-brown — 10 to 12 minutes. Slide the puffed pancake out of the casserole on to a warmed serving plate. Cut the pancake into four wedges and serve it immediately with the rum-pineapple topping.

# Potato Griddle Cakes with Apple-Mustard Compote

Serves 8
Working time: about 45 minutes
Total time: about 1 hour and 10 minutes

Calories **205**
Protein **3g**
Cholesterol **40mg**
Total fat **4g**
Saturated fat **2g**
Sodium **160mg**

| | | |
|---|---|---|
| 1 | potato (about 250 g/½ lb), peeled and diced | 1 |
| 1 | egg, separated, plus 1 egg white | 1 |
| 1 tsp | caster sugar | 1 tsp |
| ¼ tsp | salt | ¼ tsp |
| ⅛ tsp | grated nutmeg | ⅛ tsp |
| 75 g | plain flour | 2½ oz |
| **Apple-mustard compote** | | |
| 6 | firm, tart apples that will hold their shape when cooked, quartered, cored, peeled and cut into eighths | 6 |
| 6 tbsp | sugar | 6 tbsp |
| 6 tbsp | unsweetened apple juice | 6 tbsp |
| 30 g | unsalted butter | 1 oz |
| 40 g | sultanas | 1¼ oz |
| 1 | lemon, grated rind and juice | 1 |
| ½ tsp | ground cinnamon | ½ tsp |
| 2 tbsp | grainy mustard | 2 tbsp |

Put the diced potato into a saucepan and cover it with water. Bring the water to the boil, then reduce the heat, and simmer the potato until it is soft — 10 to 15 minutes.

While the potato is cooking, prepare the apple-mustard compote. Put the apples, sugar, apple juice, butter, sultanas, lemon rind and lemon juice into a heavy frying pan over medium-high heat. Cook the mixture, stirring frequently, until the apples are heated through and tender — about 5 minutes. Stir in the cinnamon and mustard, and keep the compote warm while you make the griddle cakes. (If you like, you can make the compote a day ahead and reheat it.)

Drain the cooked potato, reserving ¼ litre (8 fl oz) of the cooking liquid. Put the potato into a bowl and mash it with a potato masher or a fork until it is smooth; alternatively, work the potato through a sieve. Stir in the reserved cooking liquid and let the mashed potato cool to lukewarm.

Stir the egg yolk, sugar, salt and nutmeg into the mashed potato. Sift in the flour and stir the mixture just until it is blended.

Put the egg whites into a bowl and beat them until they form soft peaks. Stir about a quarter of the egg whites into the potato mixture and then gently fold in the remaining egg whites.

Heat a large griddle or frying pan *(box, page 55)* over medium heat until a few drops of cold water dance when sprinkled on the surface. Spoon about 4 tablespoons of the batter at a time on to the griddle or pan and use the back of the spoon to spread the batter into rounds. Cook the griddle cakes until they are covered with bubbles and the undersides are golden — 1 to 3 minutes. Flip the cakes and cook them until the second sides are lightly browned — about 1 minute more. Transfer the cakes to a platter and keep them warm while you cook the remaining batter. Serve the griddle cakes immediately with the apple-mustard compote.

# Cornmeal Buttermilk Pancakes

Serves 6
Working (and total) time: about 20 minutes

Calories **285**
Protein **8g**
Cholesterol **95mg**
Total fat **7g**
Saturated fat **1g**
Sodium **245mg**

| | | |
|---|---|---|
| 175 g | plain flour | 6 oz |
| 3 tbsp | caster sugar | 3 tbsp |
| ½ tsp | bicarbonate of soda | ½ tsp |
| ¼ tsp | salt | ¼ tsp |
| 125 g | cornmeal | 4 oz |
| 2 | eggs | 2 |
| 35 cl | buttermilk | 12 fl oz |
| 2 tbsp | safflower oil | 2 tbsp |

Sift the flour, sugar, bicarbonate of soda and salt into a bowl; stir in the cornmeal. In another bowl whisk together the eggs, buttermilk and oil.

Pour the buttermilk mixture into the dry ingredients and whisk them quickly together until they are just blended; do not overmix.

Heat a large griddle or frying pan *(box, page 55)* over medium heat until a few drops of cold water dance when sprinkled on the surface. Drop 2 tablespoons of the batter on to the hot griddle or pan, and use the back of the spoon to spread the batter into a round. Fill the pan with pancakes; cook them until the tops are covered with bubbles and the undersides are golden— 1 to 2 minutes. Flip the pancakes over and cook them until the second sides are lightly browned — about 1 minute more. Transfer the pancakes to a platter and keep them warm while you cook the remaining batter.

Serve the pancakes immediately, accompanied by a topping of your choice.

# Orange French Toast

Serves 8
Working time: about 30 minutes
Total time: about 45 minutes

Calories **385**
Protein **10g**
Cholesterol **105mg**
Total fat **6g**
Saturated fat **1g**
Sodium **375mg**

| | | |
|---|---|---|
| 25 g | sliced almonds | ¾ oz |
| 1 | loaf (about 500 g/1 lb) unsliced day-old dense white or wholemeal bread, ends trimmed | 1 |
| 3 | eggs, plus 3 egg whites | 3 |
| 45 g | caster sugar | 1½ oz |
| ¼ tsp | salt | ¼ tsp |
| 1 | orange, grated rind only | 1 |
| 1 tsp | pure vanilla extract | 1 tsp |
| 35 cl | fresh orange juice | 12 fl oz |
| **Orange syrup** | | |
| 175 g | light brown sugar | 6 oz |
| 175 g | frozen orange juice concentrate | 6 oz |

Preheat the oven to 190°C (375°F or Mark 5). In a small, heavy frying pan set over medium heat, toast the almonds, stirring constantly, until they are golden-brown — about 5 minutes. Remove the almonds from the pan and set them aside.

Cut the bread into 16 slices about 1 cm (½ in) thick. In a shallow dish, whisk together the eggs, egg whites, caster sugar, salt, orange rind and vanilla extract, then stir in the fresh orange juice.

Dip the bread slices into the juice mixture, turning them once or twice until they are thoroughly soaked with the liquid; transfer the slices to a large plate or baking sheet as you work. After all the slices have been soaked, dribble any remaining liquid over them.

Heat a large griddle or frying pan (box, page 55) over medium heat until a few drops of cold water dance when sprinkled on the surface. Cook the slices until the undersides are golden — about 3 minutes. Turn the slices and cook them until the second sides are lightly browned — 2 to 3 minutes more. Transfer the French toast to a clean baking sheet. Brown the remaining slices and transfer them to the baking sheet, too. Bake the French toast until it is cooked through and has puffed up — about 10 minutes.

While the toast is baking, make the orange syrup. Pour ¼ litre (8 fl oz) of water into a small saucepan and stir in the brown sugar; bring the liquid to the boil. Reduce the heat to medium low and simmer the mixture to dissolve the sugar — about 1 minute. Add the orange juice concentrate and cook the syrup, stirring, until it is heated through — about 1 minute more. Pour the syrup into a pitcher.

Divide the French toast among eight warmed plates and sprinkle each serving with some toasted almonds. Pass the syrup separately.

# Rye Griddle Cakes

Serves 8
Working (and total) time: about 30 minutes

Calories **155**
Protein **10g**
Cholesterol **80mg**
Total fat **3g**
Saturated fat **1g**
Sodium **315mg**

| | | |
|---|---|---|
| 2 | eggs, plus 2 egg whites | 2 |
| 15 cl | semi-skimmed milk | ¼ pint |
| 2 | large spring onions, trimmed and finely chopped | 2 |
| ¼ tsp | salt | ¼ tsp |
| | freshly ground black pepper | |
| 250 g | fresh dark rye breadcrumbs (made from about ½ loaf of dark rye bread) | 8 oz |
| **Accompaniments** | | |
| 175 g | yogurt cheese (recipe, page 50) | 6 oz |
| 1 tbsp | red lumpfish caviare | 1 tbsp |
| 1 | spring onion, sliced diagonally | 1 |
| 1 | lemon, thinly sliced (optional) | 1 |

Whisk together the eggs, egg whites, milk, finely chopped spring onions, salt and a generous grinding of pepper in a bowl. Stir in the breadcrumbs to make a smooth mixture.

Heat a large griddle or frying pan (box, page 55) over medium heat until a few drops of water dance when sprinkled on the surface. Drop the batter 1 generous tablespoon at a time on to the griddle or pan, and use the back of the spoon to spread the batter into ovals. Cook the griddle cakes until they are covered with bubbles — 1 to 3 minutes. Turn each cake and cook the second side for 1 minute more. Transfer the cakes to a platter and keep them warm while you cook the remaining batter.

Accompany each serving with a dollop of yogurt cheese topped with some caviare and sliced spring onion; if you wish, garnish with a slice of lemon.

EDITOR'S NOTE: *Plain low-fat yogurt may be substituted for the yogurt cheese.*

# Griddle Cheesecakes with Cranberry Sauce

Serves 8
Working (and total) time: about 30 minutes

Calories **220**
Protein **10g**
Cholesterol **70mg**
Total fat **2g**
Saturated fat **1g**
Sodium **300mg**

| | | |
|---|---|---|
| 450 g | low-fat cottage cheese | 15 oz |
| 2 | eggs | 2 |
| 45 g | caster sugar | 1½ oz |
| 150 g | plain flour | 5 oz |
| 1 tsp | baking powder | 1 tsp |
| 1 | lemon, grated rind only | 1 |
| **Cranberry sauce** | | |
| 100 g | sugar | 3½ oz |
| 1 tbsp | cornflour | 1 tbsp |
| 35 cl | fresh orange juice | 12 fl oz |
| 200 g | fresh or frozen cranberries, picked over | 7 oz |

To make the cranberry sauce, combine the sugar and cornflour in a heavy-bottomed saucepan. Gradually pour in the orange juice, stirring continuously. Add the cranberries and bring the mixture to the boil over medium heat, stirring constantly. Reduce the heat and simmer the mixture until all the cranberries have burst — about 15 minutes. Purée the cranberry mixture in a food processor or a blender and then pass it through a sieve into a bowl. Set the sauce aside in a warm place.

Rinse out the food processor or blender and purée the cottage cheese in it. Add the eggs and blend them into the purée. Transfer the mixture to a bowl and stir in the sugar, flour and baking powder, beating just long enough to produce a smooth batter. Stir the lemon rind into the batter.

Heat a large griddle or frying pan *(box, page 55)* over medium heat until a few drops of cold water dance when sprinkled on the surface. Drop a generous tablespoon of the batter on to the hot griddle or pan, and use the back of the spoon to spread the batter to a thickness of 5 mm (¼ inch). Form several more batter rounds in the same way, then cook the griddle cheesecakes until they are covered with bubbles and the undersides are golden — about 3 minutes. Flip the cheesecakes and cook them until the second sides are lightly browned — about 1 minute more. Transfer the cheesecakes to a platter and keep them warm while you cook the remaining batter.

Serve the griddle cheesecakes accompanied by the cranberry sauce.

# Paprika Blintzes

Serves 4 as a main dish
Working time: about 50 minutes
Total time: about 1 hour and 30 minutes (includes standing time for crêpe batter)

Calories **225**
Protein **14g**
Cholesterol **80mg**
Total fat **10g**
Saturated fat **3g**
Sodium **420mg**

| | | |
|---|---|---|
| 75 g | plain flour | 2½ oz |
| ⅛ tsp | salt | ⅛ tsp |
| 1½ tsp | paprika, preferably Hungarian | 1½ tsp |
| 1 | egg | 1 |
| 17.5 cl | semi-skimmed milk | 6 fl oz |
| 1 tbsp | virgin olive oil | 1 tbsp |
| 1½ tsp | fresh thyme, or ½ tsp dried thyme | 1½ tsp |
| ¼ tsp | safflower oil | ¼ tsp |
| **Cheese and spring onion filling** | | |
| 1½ tsp | virgin olive oil | 1½ tsp |
| 1 | garlic clove, finely chopped | 1 |
| 2 | bunches spring onions, trimmed and cut into 2.5 cm (1 inch) pieces | 2 |
| 1½ tsp | fresh thyme, or ½ tsp dried thyme | 1½ tsp |
| | freshly ground black pepper | |
| ⅛ tsp | salt | ⅛ tsp |
| 175 g | low-fat cottage cheese | 6 oz |
| 12.5 cl | plain low-fat yogurt | 4 fl oz |
| 2 tbsp | freshly grated Parmesan cheese | 2 tbsp |

To make the crêpes for the blintzes, sift the flour, salt and paprika into a bowl. Make a well in the centre, then add the egg, milk, olive oil and thyme. Whisk the mixture, gradually incorporating the flour. Cover the bowl and let it stand for 1 hour, or refrigerate it overnight. If the batter has thickened at the end of the refrigeration period, stir in water, 1 tablespoon at a time, to restore the original consistency.

To make the filling, heat the olive oil in a heavy-bottomed saucepan over medium-high heat. Add the garlic, spring onions, thyme, some pepper and the salt. Cook, stirring frequently, until the spring onions are soft — 4 to 5 minutes. Transfer the mixture to a bowl.

Put the cottage cheese, yogurt and Parmesan cheese into a food processor or a blender and purée them. Add the puréed mixture to the spring onions. Stir the mixture well, then set it aside.

Heat a 15 cm (6 in) crêpe pan or a non-stick frying pan over medium-high heat. Add the ¼ teaspoon of safflower oil and spread it over the entire surface with a paper towel. Ladle about 3 tablespoons of the crêpe batter into the hot pan and immediately swirl the pan to coat the bottom with a thin, even layer of batter. Pour any excess batter back into the bowl. Cook the crêpe until the bottom is browned — about 2 minutes and 30 seconds. Lift the edge with a spatula and turn the crêpe over. Cook the crêpe on the second side until it, too, is browned — 15 to 30 seconds. Slide the crêpe on to a plate. Repeat the process with the remaining batter to form eight crêpes in all.

Preheat the oven to 200°C (400°F or Mark 6). Spoon about 4 tablespoons of the cheese and spring onion mixture on to a crêpe near its edge. Fold the edge of the crêpe over the filling, then fold in the sides of the crêpe, forming an envelope round the filling. Roll up the crêpes to enclose the filling completely. Repeat the process with the remaining crêpes and filling to form eight blintzes. Lightly oil a baking sheet, set the blintzes on it, and bake them until they are crisp and lightly browned round the edges — about 8 minutes. Serve the blintzes immediately.

# Buckwheat Crêpes with Mushroom-Tomato Filling

Serves 8 as a main dish
Working time: about 1 hour
Total time: about 2 hours
(includes standing time for crêpe batter)

Calories **175**
Protein **10g**
Cholesterol **45mg**
Total fat **6g**
Saturated fat **2g**
Sodium **225mg**

| | | |
|---|---|---|
| 1 | egg | 1 |
| 35 cl | semi-skimmed milk | 12 fl oz |
| ½ tsp | caster sugar | ½ tsp |
| ⅛ tsp | salt | ⅛ tsp |
| 15 g | unsalted butter, melted | ½ oz |
| 60 g | buckwheat flour | 2 oz |
| 75 g | plain flour | 2½ oz |
| ¼ tsp | safflower oil | ¼ tsp |
| **Mushroom-tomato filling** | | |
| 1 tbsp | safflower oil | 1 tbsp |
| 500 g | mushrooms, wiped clean, trimmed and quartered | 1 lb |
| 2 | shallots, thinly sliced | 2 |
| 1 tbsp | plain flour | 1 tbsp |
| 12.5 cl | unsalted brown stock, or ¼ litre (8 fl oz) unsalted chicken stock reduced by half (recipes, page 138) | 4 fl oz |
| 4 tbsp | dry vermouth | 4 tbsp |
| 4 | garlic cloves, finely chopped | 4 |
| 2 | large tomatoes, skinned, seeded and chopped | 2 |
| 1 tbsp | Dijon mustard | 1 tbsp |
| 2 tbsp | chopped parsley | 2 tbsp |
| | parsley sprigs, for garnish | |
| **Creamy cheese topping** | | |
| 225 g | low-fat cottage cheese | 7½ oz |
| 2 tbsp | buttermilk | 2 tbsp |

Put the egg into a bowl and beat it until it is light and foamy. Whisk in the milk, sugar, salt and butter, and then gradually whisk in the two flours. Cover the bowl and let it stand for 1 hour. (Alternatively, you may refrigerate the batter, covered, overnight.) If the batter has thickened at the end of the refrigeration period, stir in additional milk, 1 tablespoon at a time, until the batter has thinned to its original consistency.

While the batter is resting, make the mushroom-tomato filling. Heat the oil in a heavy frying pan over medium-high heat. Add the mushrooms and shallots and sauté them until the mushrooms begin to exude their liquid — about 5 minutes.

Add the flour to the mushrooms and cook the mixture, stirring, for 1 minute. Add the brown stock or reduced chicken stock, vermouth, garlic and half of the tomatoes; reduce the heat and simmer the mixture for 3 minutes, stirring frequently. Stir in the mustard and

chopped parsley and remove the pan from the heat.

When the crêpe batter is ready, heat a 15 cm (6 inch) crêpe pan or non-stick frying pan over medium-high heat. Add the ¼ teaspoon of oil and spread it over the entire surface with a paper towel. Put about 3 table-spoons of the batter into the hot pan and immediately swirl the pan to coat the bottom with a thin, even layer of batter. Pour any excess batter back into the bowl. Cook the crêpe until the bottom is browned — about 1 minute. Lift the edge with a spatula and turn the crêpe over. Cook the crêpe on the second side until it, too, is browned — 15 to 30 seconds. Slide the crêpe on to a plate. Repeat the process with the remaining batter, brushing the pan lightly with more oil if the crêpes begin to stick. Stack the cooked crêpes on the plate as you go. Cover the crêpes with a towel and set them aside. There should be about 16 crêpes.

Preheat the oven to 180°C (350°F or Mark 4). Spoon 2 tablespoons of the filling down the centre of a crêpe. Roll the crêpe to enclose the filling, then transfer it to a lightly oiled shallow baking dish. Con-tinue filling and rolling the remaining crêpes, trans-ferring them to the baking dish as you work. Bake the filled crêpes for 15 minutes.

While the crêpes are baking, make the cheese top-ping. Put the cottage cheese into a food processor or a blender and purée it. Add the buttermilk and process the mixture until it is blended.

Garnish the crêpes with the remaining chopped tomato and the parsley sprigs and serve them with the cheese topping.

# Toasted Turkey and Provolone Sandwiches with Strawberry-Cranberry Jam

Serves 6 as a main dish
Working (and total) time: about 45 minutes

Calories **445**
Protein **31g**
Cholesterol **60mg**
Total fat **12g**
Saturated fat **6g**
Sodium **580mg**

| 12 | slices white sandwich bread | 12 |
|---|---|---|
| 2 tsp | Dijon mustard | 2 tsp |
| 350 g | roast turkey breast meat, sliced | 12 oz |
| 175 g | provolone cheese, sliced | 6 oz |
| 1 | large red onion, thinly sliced | 1 |
| 12.5 cl | semi-skimmed milk | 4 fl oz |
| 1 | egg white | 1 |
| ¼ tsp | ground white pepper | ¼ tsp |
| **Strawberry-cranberry jam** | | |
| 100 g | fresh or frozen cranberries | 3½ oz |
| 1 | orange, rind julienned, juice reserved | 1 |
| 1 | lemon, rind julienned, juice reserved | 1 |
| 100 g | sugar | 3½ oz |
| 175 g | fresh strawberries, hulled and halved, or 250 g (8 oz) frozen whole strawberries, thawed and halved | 6 oz |

To make the jam, combine the cranberries, orange rind and juice, lemon rind and juice, and sugar in a non-reactive saucepan. Bring the mixture to the boil, reduce the heat, and simmer the fruit for 5 minutes. Add the strawberries to the saucepan, stir well, and cook the jam for an additional 5 minutes. Transfer the jam to a bowl and chill it.

Preheat the oven to 180°C (350°F or Mark 4).

Lay six of the bread slices out on a work surface and brush them with the mustard. Divide the turkey, provolone cheese and onion among these six slices. Set the remaining slices of bread on top.

In a small bowl, whisk together the milk, egg white and pepper. Brush both sides of the sandwiches with this mixture. Heat a large griddle or frying pan *(box, page 55)* over medium heat until a few drops of cold water dance when sprinkled on the surface. Put the sandwiches on the griddle or in the pan and cook them until the undersides are well browned — about 5 minutes. Turn the sandwiches and cook them until the second sides are browned — 2 to 3 minutes more. Serve the sandwiches immediately, accompanied by the jam.

# Puffy Fruit Omelette

Serves 4 as a main dish
Working (and total) time: about 40 minutes

Calories **200**
Protein **10g**
Cholesterol **140mg**
Total fat **5g**
Saturated fat **1g**
Sodium **250mg**

| | | |
|---|---|---|
| 2 | eggs, separated, plus 2 egg whites | 2 |
| 2 tbsp | plain flour | 2 tbsp |
| ½ tsp | baking powder | ½ tsp |
| ⅛ tsp | salt | ⅛ tsp |
| 12.5 cl | semi-skimmed milk | 4 fl oz |
| 15 g | caster sugar | ½ oz |
| 1 tsp | safflower oil | 1 tsp |
| 1 | red eating apple, quartered, cored and cut into 1 cm (½ inch) pieces | 1 |
| 1 | pear, quartered, cored and cut into 1 cm (½ inch) pieces | 1 |
| 1 tsp | fresh lemon juice | 1 tsp |
| ¼ tsp | ground cinnamon | ¼ tsp |
| 2 tbsp | raspberry jam | 2 tbsp |
| 2 tbsp | unsweetened apple juice | 2 tbsp |

Preheat the oven to 230°C (450°F or Mark 8). In a bowl, whisk together the egg yolks, flour, baking powder, salt and 3 tablespoons of the milk until the mixture is well blended — 5 to 7 minutes. Whisk in the remaining milk.

In another bowl, beat the egg whites with 3 teaspoons of the sugar until they form soft peaks. Stir half of the whites into the yolk mixture and then gently fold in the remaining whites just until the mixture is blended; do not overmix. Set the egg mixture aside.

Heat the oil in a large, shallow fireproof casserole over medium-high heat. Add the apple and the pear, the remaining sugar, the lemon juice and the cinnamon and cook the fruit, stirring frequently, until it is tender — about 5 minutes. Remove the casserole from the heat and pour the egg mixture over the fruit; smooth the top of the mixture with a spatula. Place the casserole in the oven and bake the omelette until the top is golden-brown — 10 to 15 minutes.

While the omelette is baking, mix together the raspberry jam and the unsweetened apple juice in a small dish. When the omelette is ready, dribble this syrup over it, slice it into quarters and serve immediately.

## Frittata with Mozzarella Cheese

Serves 4 as a main dish
Working (and total) time: about 35 minutes

Calories **170**
Protein **11g**
Cholesterol **85mg**
Total fat **11g**
Saturated fat **4g**
Sodium **320mg**

| | | |
|---|---|---|
| 1 | egg, plus 2 egg whites | 1 |
| ¼ tsp | salt | ¼ tsp |
| | freshly ground black pepper | |
| 4 tbsp | low-fat ricotta cheese | 4 tbsp |
| 1½ tbsp | virgin olive oil | 1½ tbsp |
| 90 g | mushrooms, wiped clean and sliced | 3 oz |
| 2 | garlic cloves, finely chopped | 2 |
| 1½ tsp | fresh thyme, or ½ tsp dried thyme | 1½ tsp |
| 3 | spring onions, trimmed and cut into 1 cm (½ inch) pieces, white and green parts separated | 3 |
| 250 g | courgettes, cut into bâtons | 8 oz |
| 1 | sweet red pepper, seeded, deribbed and sliced into thin strips | 1 |
| 1½ tsp | fresh lemon juice | 1½ tsp |
| 2 tbsp | freshly grated Parmesan cheese | 2 tbsp |
| 60 g | low-fat mozzarella, cut into thin strips | 2 oz |

In a bowl, whisk together the egg, egg whites, ⅛ teaspoon of the salt, some pepper, the ricotta and ½ tablespoon of the oil, and set the mixture aside.

Preheat the grill. Heat the remaining tablespoon of oil in a large, shallow non-stick fireproof casserole over high heat. Add the mushrooms, garlic, thyme, the white parts of the spring onions and some pepper. Cook the vegetable mixture until the mushrooms are lightly browned — 2 to 3 minutes. Add the courgettes, red pepper, the remaining ⅛ teaspoon of salt and the lemon juice, and cook the mixture, stirring frequently, until the vegetables are tender and all of the liquid has evaporated — about 5 minutes.

Remove the casserole from the heat and stir the spring onion greens and the Parmesan cheese into the vegetable mixture. Press the vegetables into an even layer and pour in the egg mixture. Cook the frittata over medium heat for 1 minute. Sprinkle the mozzarella evenly over the frittata and place the casserole under the preheated grill. Grill the frittata until the cheese begins to brown — 2 to 3 minutes. Slide the frittata on to a warm serving plate and cut into quarters. Serve the frittata immediately.

## Omelettes Stuffed with Seafood and Bean Sprouts

Serves 4
Working (and total) time: about 35 minutes

Calories **160**
Protein **13g**
Cholesterol **105mg**
Total fat **8g**
Saturated fat **1g**
Sodium **85mg**

| | | |
|---|---|---|
| 3 tbsp | rice vinegar | 3 tbsp |
| 1 tbsp | caster sugar | 1 tbsp |
| 1 tbsp | fresh lemon juice | 1 tbsp |
| 250 g | bean sprouts | 8 oz |
| 125 g | French beans, trimmed and cut diagonally into thin slices | 4 oz |
| 1 tbsp | plus 2 tsp safflower oil | 1 tbsp |
| 1 tsp | curry powder | 1 tsp |
| | freshly ground black pepper | |
| 60 g | cooked peeled prawns, chopped | 2 oz |
| 125 g | sole or plaice fillets, cut into strips | 4 oz |
| 2 | spring onions, thinly sliced | 2 |
| 1 | egg, plus 3 egg whites | 1 |

Mix the vinegar, 2 teaspoons of the sugar and the lemon juice in a small bowl and set it aside.

Blanch the bean sprouts and the beans in 1 litre (2 pints) of boiling water for 30 seconds. Drain the vegetables and refresh them under cold running water. Squeeze the vegetables in your hands to extract as much liquid as possible. Set the vegetables aside.

Heat 1 teaspoon of the oil in a large, non-stick frying pan over medium-high heat. Add the bean sprouts and beans and cook, stirring frequently, for 2 minutes. Add ½ teaspoon of the curry powder, half the vinegar mixture and a generous grinding of pepper. Stir well and continue cooking until all the liquid has evaporated — about 2 minutes. Transfer to a bowl and set aside.

Return the pan to the heat and pour in 1 tablespoon of the oil. Add the prawns, sole or plaice, and spring onions and cook the mixture, stirring frequently, for 1 minute. Add the remaining vinegar mixture, then stir in ▶

the vegetable mixture, and cook them, stirring frequently, until all of the liquid has evaporated — 2 to 4 minutes. Set the seafood and vegetables aside.

In a bowl, whisk together the egg, egg whites, the remaining curry powder, the remaining sugar, the remaining oil and some pepper. With a paper towel, wipe out the non-stick frying pan that the seafood and vegetables were cooked in and heat the pan over medium heat. Pour a scant 4 tablespoons of the egg mixture into the hot pan and swirl it around. Cook the omelette for 30 seconds, turn it over, and cook it for 10 seconds more. Transfer the omelette to a warm plate. Repeat the process with the remaining egg mixture to make four thin omelettes.

Take a quarter of the filling and spread it over one half of one omelette. Fold the omelette over and repeat the process with the remaining omelettes and filling. Serve the filled omelettes immediately.

# Turkey, Apple and Champagne Patties

Serves 10 as a main dish
Working (and total) time: about 45 minutes

Calories **110**
Protein **14g**
Cholesterol **30mg**
Total fat **2g**
Saturated fat **1g**
Sodium **160mg**

| | | |
|---|---|---|
| 1 | red apple, cored and finely chopped | 1 |
| 1 | onion, finely chopped | 1 |
| 90 g | fine dry breadcrumbs | 3 oz |
| 12.5 cl | champagne or other sparkling dry white wine | 4 fl oz |
| 500 g | turkey breast meat, minced | 1 lb |
| 125 g | pork fillet, trimmed of fat and minced | 4 oz |
| ½ tsp | salt | ½ tsp |
| | freshly ground black pepper | |

Put the apple and onion into a non-stick frying pan over low heat and cook them, covered, until they are soft — about 4 minutes.

Combine the breadcrumbs and the wine in a bowl. Add the turkey, pork, salt, some pepper and the apple-onion mixture, kneading the ingredients with your hands to mix them well. Shape the sausage meat into 20 patties about 1 cm (½ inch) thick.

Heat a large, non-stick frying pan over medium heat and put half the patties into it. Cook them until the undersides are brown, then turn the patties over, and brown the other sides — about 4 minutes in all. Remove the browned patties to a platter and keep them warm while you cook the others. Serve the patties at once.

# Spaghetti Omelette

Serves 8 as a side dish
Working (and total) time: about 1 hour

Calories **120**
Protein **7g**
Cholesterol **6mg**
Total fat **3g**
Saturated fat **1g**
Sodium **260mg**

| | | |
|---|---|---|
| 800 g | canned whole tomatoes, with their juice | 1¾ lb |
| 125 g | spaghetti, spaghettini or linguine | 4 oz |
| ½ tsp | salt | ½ tsp |
| 2 | egg whites | 2 |
| 12.5 cl | semi-skimmed milk | 4 fl oz |
| 1 tbsp | chopped parsley | 1 tbsp |
| 3 tbsp | freshly grated Parmesan cheese | 3 tbsp |
| | freshly ground black pepper | |
| 1 tsp | grated lemon rind | 1 tsp |
| 2 tsp | virgin olive oil | 2 tsp |
| 60 g | low-fat mozzarella cheese, grated | 2 oz |

Put the tomatoes into a heavy-bottomed non-reactive saucepan. Simmer the tomatoes, stirring them occasionally to prevent them from sticking, until the mixture thickens — 20 to 30 minutes.

While the tomatoes are cooking, prepare the pasta. In a large pot, boil 2 litres (3½ pints) of water with 1 teaspoon of salt. Add the pasta. Start testing the pasta after 8 minutes and cook it until it is *al dente*. Drain the cooked pasta, rinse it under cold running water and then drain it again, thoroughly.

In a large bowl, beat together the egg whites, milk, parsley, Parmesan, a generous grinding of pepper, the ½ teaspoon of salt and the lemon rind. Toss the pasta with the egg white mixture.

Heat a 22 cm (9 inch) non-stick frying pan over medium-high heat. Add the oil, let it heat for 10 seconds and then swirl the pan to evenly coat the bottom with the oil. Put half of the pasta mixture into the pan; use a rubber spatula to smooth the mixture into an even layer. Reduce the heat to medium. Sprinkle the mozzarella over the pasta mixture and cover it with the remaining mixture. Let the omelette cook slowly until it is firm and the bottom and sides are browned — about 8 minutes.

Slide the omelette on to a plate. Invert the pan over the plate and turn both over together. Cook the second side of the omelette until it, too, is browned — approximately 8 minutes longer.

While the omelette is cooking, make the tomato sauce: work the cooked tomatoes through a sieve and discard the seeds. Keep the tomato sauce warm.

To serve the omelette, slide it on to a warmed serving platter. Cut the omelette into eight wedges and serve it immediately, passing the tomato sauce separately.

# Greek-Style Chicken and Rice Casserole

Serves 8 as a main dish
Working time: about 30 minutes
Total time: about 1 hour

Calories **275**
Protein **17g**
Cholesterol **50mg**
Total fat **11g**
Saturated fat **3g**
Sodium **245mg**

| | | |
|---|---|---|
| 2 tbsp | safflower oil | 2 tbsp |
| 8 | chicken thighs, skinned | 8 |
| 175 g | long-grain rice | 6 oz |
| 1 | onion, chopped | 1 |
| 4 | garlic cloves, finely chopped | 4 |
| ¼ litre | unsalted chicken stock (recipe, page 138) | 8 fl oz |
| 800 g | canned whole tomatoes | 1¾ lb |
| 3 tbsp | chopped fresh oregano, or 2 tsp dried oregano | 3 tbsp |
| 1 tbsp | fresh thyme, or 1 tsp dried thyme | 1 tbsp |
| 12 | oil-cured olives, stoned and quartered, or 12 stoned black olives, coarsely chopped | 12 |
| 30 g | feta cheese, rinsed and crumbled | 1 oz |

Heat the oil in a large, heavy fireproof casserole over medium-high heat. Add four of the thighs and cook them until they are lightly browned — about 4 minutes on each side. Remove the first four thighs and brown the other four. Set all the thighs aside.

Reduce the heat to medium and add the rice, onion, garlic and 4 tablespoons of the stock. Cook the mixture, stirring constantly, until the onion is translucent — about 4 minutes. Add the remaining stock, the tomatoes, the oregano and the thyme. Push the thighs down into the rice mixture. Bring the liquid to the boil, reduce the heat, and simmer the chicken, tightly covered, until the rice is tender — 20 to 30 minutes.

Stir the olives into the chicken and rice, and serve the casserole with the feta cheese on top.

# Lean Beef Sausages

Serves 4 as a main dish
Working time: about 20 minutes
Total time: about 40 minutes

Calories **100**
Protein **14g**
Cholesterol **35mg**
Total fat **4g**
Saturated fat **1g**
Sodium **125mg**

| | | |
|---|---|---|
| 250 g | beef topside, trimmed of fat and minced | 8 oz |
| 12.5 cl | unsalted brown stock (recipe, page 138) | 4 fl oz |
| 2 tbsp | fresh breadcrumbs | 2 tbsp |
| ½ tsp | grated lemon rind | ½ tsp |
| ½ tsp | finely chopped garlic | ½ tsp |
| 1 tsp | chopped fresh sage, or | 1 tsp |
| | ¼ tsp crumbled dried sage | |
| ½ tsp | paprika | ½ tsp |
| 1 | egg white | 1 |
| ⅛ tsp | salt | ⅛ tsp |
| | freshly ground black pepper | |

In a large bowl, mix together the beef, brown stock, breadcrumbs, lemon rind, garlic, sage, paprika, egg white, salt and some pepper.

Arrange half of the beef mixture in a line on a piece of strong aluminium foil about 30 cm (12 inches) long. Form one sausage following the technique shown opposite. Using the remaining meat mixture, shape a second sausage.

Pour enough water into a large pan to fill it about 2.5 cm (1 inch) deep. Set a vegetable steamer in the pan and put the sausages into it. Cover the pan and bring the water to the boil. Steam the sausages until they are firm — 7 to 10 minutes. Remove the steamer from the pan and let the sausages cool in the foil. Remove the foil from the sausages and cut them in half crosswise.

Heat a non-stick frying pan over medium-high heat, put the sausages into the pan and cook them until they are well browned on all sides — 4 to 5 minutes in all. Serve the sausages at once.

## Making a Sausage

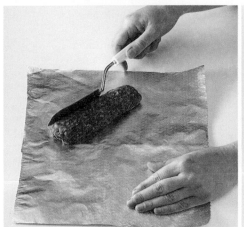

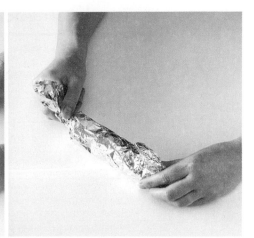

**1** *SHAPING THE MEAT. Lay a piece of strong aluminium foil on a work surface. Place the prepared meat mixture in the amount specified in the recipe near the edge of the foil. Pat the meat into a cylindrical shape with a spatula.*

**2** *WRAPPING THE MIXTURE. Fold the flap of foil over the sausage. Holding the spatula against the edge of the meat, exert pressure to force out extra air and to compact the sausage. Roll the bundle forwards, wrapping the sausage tightly as you go.*

**3** *SECURING THE PARCEL. To help the sausage hold its shape and to prevent water from seeping into it during the cooking, twist the two ends of the foil and fold them over.*

# Lentil and Curly Endive Salad

Serves 8 as a side dish
Working time: about 20 minutes
Total time: about 1 hour

Calories **115**
Protein **6g**
Cholesterol **0mg**
Total fat **3g**
Saturated fat **0g**
Sodium **75mg**

| | | |
|---|---|---|
| 2 | ripe tomatoes, halved, seeded and cut into 1 cm (½ inch) pieces | 2 |
| 250 g | lentils, picked over | 8 oz |
| ¼ tsp | salt | ¼ tsp |
| | freshly ground black pepper | |
| 1½ tbsp | virgin olive oil | 1½ tbsp |
| ½ | head of curly endive (frisée), washed, dried and sliced into 2.5 cm (1 inch) pieces | ½ |
| 1 tsp | honey | 1 tsp |
| 4 tbsp | red wine vinegar | 4 tbsp |

Put the tomatoes into a strainer and let them drain; set the strainer aside.

Rinse the lentils and put them into a saucepan with 1 litre (2 pints) of water. Bring the water to the boil, then reduce the heat, and simmer the lentils until they are tender — 25 to 40 minutes. Drain the lentils and then transfer them to a bowl. Toss them with the salt and some pepper and set the bowl aside.

Heat ½ tablespoon of the oil in a large, heavy frying pan over high heat. Add the endive and some pepper and cook the mixture, stirring constantly, just until the endive has wilted — about 1 minute. Put the endive into the strainer with the tomatoes.

Whisk the remaining tablespoon of oil, the honey, vinegar and some pepper in a large bowl. Add the tomatoes, endive and lentils and toss the salad well. You can either serve the salad immediately or let it cool to room temperature.

# Four-Vegetable Kasha Salad

Serves 8 as a side dish
Working time: about 30 minutes
Total time: about 45 minutes

Calories **100**
Protein **4g**
Cholesterol **0mg**
Total fat **4g**
Saturated fat **1g**
Sodium **65mg**

| | | |
|---|---|---|
| 200 g | toasted buckwheat groats (kasha) | 7 oz |
| 1 | egg white | 1 |
| 2 tbsp | virgin olive oil | 2 tbsp |
| ⅛ tsp | salt | ⅛ tsp |
| ½ litre | unsalted chicken stock (recipe, page 138) or water | 16 fl oz |
| 750 g | fresh peas, shelled, or frozen peas, thawed | 1½ lb |
| 1 | sweet red pepper, seeded, deribbed and cut into 1 cm (½ inch) pieces | 1 |
| 3 | spring onions, trimmed and cut diagonally into 1 cm (½ inch) pieces | 3 |
| 60 g | celery, diced | 2 oz |
| ¼ tsp | cayenne pepper | ¼ tsp |
| 3 tbsp | sherry vinegar or red wine vinegar | 3 tbsp |

Mix the buckwheat groats with the egg white in a small bowl. Heat ½ tablespoon of the oil in a large, heavy-bottomed saucepan over medium heat. Add the moistened buckwheat groats to the saucepan, and cook, stirring constantly, until the grains have separated and the mixture is dry — about 3 minutes. Add the salt and the stock or water. Bring the mixture to the boil, reduce the heat, and simmer, covered, until all of the liquid is absorbed and the groats are tender — approximately 20 minutes.

While the buckwheat groats are cooking, prepare the vegetables. If you are using fresh peas, boil them until they are tender — 5 to 7 minutes. (Frozen peas do not require cooking for this recipe.) Drain the peas and put them, together with the red pepper, spring onions, celery and cayenne pepper, into a large serving bowl. Stir in the vinegar and the remaining oil. When the buckwheat groats are ready, add them to the vegetables and toss the salad well. Serve the salad either at room temperature or chilled.

# Broccoli and Ricotta Pie

Serves 6 as a main dish
Working time: about 1 hour
Total time: about 2 hours

Calories **325**
Protein **17g**
Cholesterol **65mg**
Total fat **8g**
Saturated fat **3g**
Sodium **285mg**

| | | |
|---|---|---|
| 1 tbsp | easy-blend dried yeast | 1 tbsp |
| 375 g | strong plain flour | 13 oz |
| ¼ tsp | salt | ¼ tsp |
| 1 tbsp | virgin olive oil | 1 tbsp |
| 250 g | onion, chopped | 8 oz |
| ½ tsp | caraway seeds, or 2 tsp dried dill | ½ tsp |
| 1 | egg, plus 2 egg whites | 1 |
| 175 g | low-fat ricotta cheese | 6 oz |
| 17.5 cl | semi-skimmed milk | 6 fl oz |
| | freshly ground black pepper | |
| ⅛ tsp | grated nutmeg | ⅛ tsp |
| 30 g | mild back bacon, finely chopped | 1 oz |
| 1 tbsp | cornmeal | 1 tbsp |
| 350 g | broccoli florets, blanched in boiling water for 1 minute, drained | 12 oz |
| 2 tbsp | freshly grated Parmesan cheese | 2 tbsp |

In a large bowl, mix the yeast with 140 g (5 oz) of the flour and ⅛ teaspoon of the salt. Heat 17.5 cl (6 fl oz) of water in a saucepan just until it is hot to the touch (43°C/110°F). Pour the hot water into the flour mixture and stir the dough vigorously with a wooden spoon. Stir in 1 teaspoon of the oil and another 140 g (5 oz) of the flour. Transfer the dough to a floured surface and begin to knead it. If the dough seems too sticky, gradually add the remaining flour; if it seems too dry, add water, 1 teaspoon at a time, as required. Knead the dough until it is smooth and elastic — about 10 minutes. Transfer the dough to an oiled bowl, turn the dough once to coat it with the oil, and cover the bowl

with a damp towel or plastic film. Set the bowl in a warm, draught-free place and let the dough rise until it has doubled in volume — about 30 minutes.

While the dough is rising, heat the remaining 2 teaspoons of oil in a heavy frying pan over medium-high heat. Add the onion and the caraway seeds or dill and cook the mixture, stirring frequently, until the onion is lightly browned — about 10 minutes. Remove the pan from the heat and set it aside.

Whisk the egg and the egg whites in a large bowl. Whisk in the ricotta, the milk, the remaining ⅛ teaspoon of salt, some freshly ground black pepper, the nutmeg and the mild back bacon. Stir in half of the onion mixture and set the bowl aside.

Preheat the oven to 200°C (400°F or Mark 6). After the dough has finished rising, knock it back. Knead the remaining onion mixture into the dough.

Sprinkle a 20 cm (8 inch) shallow fireproof casserole or a 28 cm (11 inch) glass pie plate with the cornmeal. Put the dough in the casserole or pie plate and, with your fingertips, gently work some of the dough towards the edge to form a 5 cm (2 inch) rim. Allow the dough to stand for 10 minutes.

Place the casserole or pie plate in the oven for 10 minutes to partially bake the dough. Remove the crust from the oven; if the edge is not 2 cm (¾ inch) higher than the flat surface of the crust, gently push the dough down to form a depression. Pour in the ricotta-egg mixture. Place the broccoli florets one at a time, bud sides up, in the filling, then sprinkle the Parmesan cheese over the surface of the pie. Return the casserole to the oven and bake the pie until the filling is set and the top is lighly browned — 35 to 40 minutes. Let the pie stand for 10 minutes before cutting it into wedges.

## Braised Chicory and Red Pepper Salad

Serves 6 as a side dish
Working time: about 30 minutes
Total time: about 2 hours (includes chilling)

Calories **40**
Protein **1g**
Cholesterol **0mg**
Total fat **2g**
Saturated fat **0g**
Sodium **110mg**

| | | |
|---|---|---|
| 2 | sweet red peppers | 2 |
| 1 tbsp | virgin olive oil | 1 tbsp |
| 500 g | chicory, trimmed and cut into 2.5 cm (1 inch) pieces | 1 lb |
| 1 tbsp | fresh thyme, or 1 tsp dried thyme | 1 tbsp |
| 1 tbsp | fresh lemon juice | 1 tbsp |
| ¼ tsp | salt | ¼ tsp |
| 3 | spring onions, trimmed and cut into 2.5 cm (1 inch) pieces | 3 |
| | freshly ground black pepper | |
| 2 tbsp | sherry vinegar, or 1 ½ tsp red wine vinegar | 2 tbsp |

To prepare the peppers, place them about 5 cm (2 inches) below a preheated grill. Grill the peppers, turning them as their sides become scorched, until their skins have blistered all over. Transfer the peppers to a bowl and cover it with plastic film, or put them in a paper bag and fold it shut; the trapped steam will make the peppers limp and loosen their skins — about 15 minutes. With a paring knife, peel off the peppers' skins in sections, peeling from top to bottom. Remove the stems, ribs and seeds from the peppers, working over a bowl to catch the juices. Strain the pepper juices into another bowl and set it aside. Slice the peppers lengthwise into 1 by 5 cm (½ by 2 inch) strips and add them to the juices.

Heat the oil in a large, heavy frying pan over medium heat. Add the chicory and the thyme and cook the mixture, stirring constantly, until the chicory begins to wilt — about 5 minutes. Stir in the lemon juice, salt, spring onions and some pepper, then cook the mixture for 3 minutes more, stirring frequently. Add the peppers with their juices, and the vinegar; continue cooking for 2 minutes. Scrape the contents of the pan into a bowl, then refrigerate the salad until it is cool — about 1½ hours. The salad may be served chilled or at room temperature.

EDITOR'S NOTE: *This dish can be made a day in advance and refrigerated until serving time.*

# Layered Bread, Tomato and Courgette Casserole

Serves 8 as a main dish
Working time: about 1 hour
Total time: about 1½ hours

Calories **200**
Protein **12g**
Cholesterol **80mg**
Total fat **5g**
Saturated fat **2g**
Sodium **375mg**

| | | |
|---|---|---|
| 2 | eggs, plus 2 egg whites | 2 |
| ¼ litre | semi-skimmed milk | 8 fl oz |
| ¼ tsp | salt | ¼ tsp |
| | freshly ground black pepper | |
| 250 g | small courgettes, cut into 5 mm (¼ inch) thick rounds | 8 oz |
| 1 | onion, chopped | 1 |
| 4 | ripe tomatoes, skinned, seeded and chopped, or 400 g (14 oz) canned whole tomatoes, drained and chopped | 4 |
| 4 tbsp | chopped parsley | 4 tbsp |
| 2 tbsp | chopped fresh basil, or 2 tsp dried basil | 2 tbsp |
| 8 | slices French bread, cut into 1 cm (½ inch) cubes | 8 |
| 125 g | low-fat mozzarella cheese, grated | 4 oz |

Whisk the eggs, egg whites, milk, salt and some pepper together in a bowl and set it aside. Preheat the oven to 180°C (350°F or Mark 5).

Put the courgettes and onion into a non-stick frying pan over low heat and cook them, covered, until they are soft — about 4 minutes. Add the tomatoes and increase the heat to high. Cook the vegetables, stirring continuously, until most of the liquid has evaporated — about 5 minutes. Remove the pan from the heat and stir in the parsley and basil.

Spoon half of the vegetable mixture into a 20 by 30 cm (8 by 12 inch) baking dish; add half of the bread cubes and sprinkle half of the cheese over the bread. Repeat the process with the remaining vegetable mixture, bread and cheese, then pour the egg mixture over all.

Bake the casserole until the egg mixture has set — about 20 minutes. Increase the oven temperature to 230°C (450°F or Mark 8) and continue baking the casserole until it is lightly browned — about 5 minutes more. Cut the casserole into eight squares and serve it hot.

# Tomato Soufflé

Serves 4 as a main dish or 8 as a side dish
Working time: about 40 minutes
Total time: about 1 hour and 40 minutes

Calories **190**
Protein **3g**
Cholesterol **70mg**
Total fat **5g**
Saturated fat **1g**
Sodium **220mg**

| | | |
|---|---|---|
| 350 g | large new potatoes, peeled and quartered | 12 oz |
| 400 g | canned whole tomatoes, seeded, the juice reserved | 14 oz |
| 1 tsp | sugar | 1 tsp |
| 1 | onion, chopped | 1 |
| 1½ tbsp | chopped fresh ginger root | 1½ tbsp |
| 2 | garlic cloves, finely chopped | 2 |
| 1 | large ripe tomato, skinned | 1 |
| 2 tbsp | plain flour | 2 tbsp |
| 1 | egg, separated, plus 4 egg whites | 1 |
| ¼ tsp | salt | ¼ tsp |
| | freshly ground black pepper | |
| 1 tbsp | virgin olive oil | 1 tbsp |

Put the potatoes into a saucepan, cover them with water, and bring to the boil. Cook the potatoes until they are tender — 15 to 20 minutes. Drain the potatoes and return them to the saucepan.

Preheat the oven to 230°C (450°F or Mark 8).

Add the canned tomatoes and their juice, the sugar, onion, ginger and garlic to the potatoes and bring the mixture to the boil. Reduce the heat and simmer the mixture, stirring frequently, until it has thickened and most of the liquid has evaporated — 15 to 20 minutes.

While the tomato mixture is simmering, prepare the fresh tomato. With a small sharp knife, cut the flesh of the tomato away from the seeds and core. Discard the seeds and core. Then cut the flesh into 5 mm (¼ inch) dice and put into a large bowl. Lightly oil a 1.5 litre (2½ pint) soufflé dish and add the flour. Invert the dish and shake out the excess flour.

Transfer the cooked tomato mixture to a food processor or blender and purée it. Pour the purée into the bowl with the diced tomato and stir in the egg yolk, salt, some pepper and the olive oil. Set the bowl aside.

Beat the egg whites in a bowl until they form soft peaks. Stir about a quarter of the beaten whites into the tomato mixture to lighten it. Gently fold in the remaining whites just until they are blended in.

Pour the soufflé mixture into the prepared dish and bake it until the soufflé has risen and the top is dark brown — 30 to 40 minutes. Serve the soufflé immediately.

# Cheddar and Vegetable Phyllo Roll

Serves 6 as a side dish
Working time: about 40 minutes
Total time: about 1 hour and 15 minutes

Calories **145**
Protein **6g**
Cholesterol **7mg**
Total fat **6g**
Saturated fat **2g**
Sodium **160mg**

| | | |
|---|---|---|
| 500 g | broccoli florets | 1 lb |
| 4 tsp | safflower oil | 4 tsp |
| 1 | shallot, finely chopped (about 2 tbsp) | 1 |
| 2 | large courgettes, grated | 2 |
| 6 tbsp | dry vermouth | 6 tbsp |
| 2 tbsp | plain flour | 2 tbsp |
| 12.5 cl | semi-skimmed milk | 4 fl oz |
| 30 g | Cheddar cheese, grated | 1 oz |
| ⅛ tsp | salt | ⅛ tsp |
| 4 | sheets phyllo dough (about 45g/1½ oz) | 4 |

Pour enough water into a saucepan to fill it 2.5 cm (1 inch) deep. Set a vegetable steamer in the pan and bring the water to the boil. Put the broccoli into the steamer, cover the pan tightly, and steam the broccoli until it is tender — about 7 minutes. When the broccoli has cooled, chop it coarsely and set it aside.

Preheat the oven to 220°C (425°F or Mark 7). Heat 2 teaspoons of the oil in a large non-stick frying pan over medium-high heat. Add the shallot and sauté it until it is translucent — about 2 minutes. Add the courgette and cook it, stirring continuously, until it is tender — about 2 minutes more. Reduce the heat to medium, add the broccoli and vermouth to the vegetables, and cook them until the vermouth has evaporated — approximately 5 minutes.

Stir the flour into the vegetables. Add the milk and continue cooking the mixture, stirring continuously, until the liquid comes to the boil. Add the cheese and salt and set the pan aside to cool.

Place the phyllo sheets, stacked on top of each other, on a work surface. Spoon the cooled vegetable mixture lengthwise down the centre of the top sheet. Fold a long side of the stack of sheets over the filling and brush the edge lightly with some of the oil. Fold the other long side over to cover the filling.

Brush both ends with about 1 teaspoon of the remaining oil. Fold up the ends to enclose the filling. Turn the phyllo roll seam side down and set it on a baking sheet. Brush the top surface of the roll with the remaining oil. Bake the roll until the phyllo is crisp — approximately 20 minutes.

*2*

# Brunches for All Occasions

Like a good piece of music, a successful meal is a harmonious composition: tastes, textures, colours and shapes combine to heighten the pleasure inherent in each individual dish. A brunch demands something more — delicious lightness. And so the 10 menus presented in this chapter are designed to satisfy your guests or family without overwhelming them with rich foods or too large a number of dishes that demand sampling and encourage indulgence. The menus are all low enough in calories to allow you to supplement the dishes — if you like, with bread, rice or potatoes.

A central idea helps give each of these menus coherence. Four are based on culinary traditions — Chinese, British, Scandinavian and the American Southwest. Four others are inspired by the seasons and the special foods then at their prime. The spring brunch, for instance, features asparagus, which is at its fleeting, succulent best in late spring and early summer. The sturdier autumn menu reflects the return of cool weather and a bountiful harvest of apples, cabbage, chestnuts and pears. The style of entertaining determines the choice of dishes for the remaining two menus, a picnic brunch and a buffet for a large group. In fact, almost all of the menus are well suited to the casual service that a buffet offers. But they could also do double duty as a sit-down meal.

Since brunches take place relatively early in the day, the menus that follow consist of dishes that for the most part can be prepared partially or completely a day or even more in advance. But make sure your refrigerator or freezer has room to accommodate the dishes, as well as any ingredients you will have to prepare on the day of the brunch.

These menus may be freely varied, according to your needs or your imagination. The Scandinavian menu, for example, provides a trio of salads, but if you are serving six people instead of the eight for which the brunch is designed, you may simply omit one of the salads. To eliminate the last-minute flurry of cooking that a stove-top bread requires, you could replace the cornmeal griddle cakes of the American Southwestern menu with the spicy sweetcorn sticks included in the first section *(page 31)*. You may also have favourite recipes from other sources that would marry well with the ones that appear here. And, if you like, you can always lift a recipe or two from any of these menus to include in a brunch of your own devising.

*Unpacked on a grassy spot, an unhurried brunch awaits picnickers. A spinach roulade is served with aubergine relish and green beans, and peach compote with orange-walnut cake and raspberry iced tea complete the meal.*

---

### PICNIC BRUNCH

*Apple-Mushroom Spinach Roulade*
*Aubergine and Pepper Relish*
*Green Beans with Garlic and Bacon*
*Fresh Peach Compote*
*Orange-Walnut Coffee Cake*
*Raspberry Iced Tea*

---

The day before this picnic brunch, bake the orange-walnut coffee cake and the spinach sponge for the roulade. Prepare the filling and fill, roll and wrap the roulade. Make the aubergine relish and the peach dessert. Prepare the bean salad to the point of adding the tomatoes. Wrap or tightly cover all the dishes. Make the raspberry tea, and refrigerate everything.

On the next day, slice the roulade, the coffee cake and the tomato garnish for the green bean salad. Pack the spinach garnish for the roulade, and put the salad, the compote and the relish into pretty containers with lids. Pack a platter for the roulade and a napkin-lined container for the cake. Pour the chilled tea into a thermos flask and, if you like, take along some ice cubes.

# Apple-Mushroom Spinach Roulade

Serves 8
Working time: about 1 hour and 15 minutes
Total time: about 1 hour and 45 minutes

Calories **125**
Protein **7g**
Cholesterol **75mg**
Total fat **5g**
Saturated fat **1g**
Sodium **270mg**

| | | |
|---|---|---|
| 350 g | spinach, washed and stemmed, or 150 g (5 oz) frozen spinach | 12 oz |
| 60 g | plain flour | 2 oz |
| 30 g | wholemeal flour | 1 oz |
| 1 tsp | baking powder | 1 tsp |
| ½ tsp | ground mace | ½ tsp |
| ¼ tsp | salt | ¼ tsp |
| | freshly ground black pepper | |
| 2 | egg yolks | 2 |
| 4 | egg whites | 4 |
| **Apple-mushroom filling** | | |
| 1 | large onion, finely chopped | 1 |
| 2 | apples, peeled, cored and chopped | 2 |
| 250 g | mushrooms, wiped clean and thinly sliced | 8 oz |
| ¼ tsp | salt | ¼ tsp |
| | freshly ground black pepper | |
| 125 g | low-fat ricotta cheese | 4 oz |

Line a 30 by 40 cm (12 by 16 inch) Swiss roll tin with parchment or greaseproof paper. Lightly butter the paper, then dust it with flour; shake off the excess flour. Set the pan aside.

If you are using fresh spinach, reserve 10 of the leaves for garnish; put the remaining leaves into a large, heavy frying pan and cook them over medium heat, stirring occasionally, just until they wilt — about 3 minutes. (The water clinging to the leaves provides enough moisture.) Transfer the spinach to a colander and let it cool. If you are using frozen spinach, thaw it but do not cook it.

Squeeze the spinach into a ball to extract as much liquid as possible. Purée the spinach in a food processor or chop it very finely by hand. Set the spinach aside.

Sift together the plain flour, wholemeal flour, baking powder, mace, salt and pepper into a small bowl. In another bowl, beat the egg yolks with an electric mixer on high until they are thick — about 4 minutes. Bring 4 tablespoons of water to the boil in a small saucepan; gradually pour the water into egg yolks, beating continuously. Beat the yolks on high speed until they are pale and very fluffy; gently stir in the spinach.

Preheat the oven to 180°C (350°F or Mark 4). In another bowl, beat the egg whites until they form soft peaks. Fold the flour mixture into the spinach-egg-yolk mixture, and then fold in the egg whites.

Spread the batter out evenly in the prepared tin. Bake the spinach sponge until it is set but still tender and moist — 8 to 10 minutes. Remove the sponge from the oven and loosen the edges with the tip of a knife. Cover the cake with a damp towel.

While the sponge is cooling, make the apple-mushroom filling. Cook the onion and the apples, covered, in a large, non-stick frying pan over low heat until the apples are very soft — about 20 minutes. Add the mushrooms and continue to cook the mixture, still covered, until the mushrooms have released their juice — about 5 minutes more. Remove the cover, increase the heat to medium high, and stir in the salt and some pepper. Simmer the mixture until almost all of the liquid has evaporated — about 3 minutes. The filling should be moist but not wet. Remove the pan from the heat. With a wooden spoon, push the ricotta through a sieve held over the pan; stir the mixture thoroughly.

To assemble the roulade, invert the Swiss roll tin so that the towel is on the bottom. Lift away the tin and peel off the paper. Spread the apple-mushroom filling on to the cake, leaving a 1 cm (½ inch) border all round. Starting at a long side, roll the sponge into a tight cylinder, using the towel to help guide the rolling process. Trim the ends, wrap the roulade tightly in aluminium foil, and refrigerate it. When you are ready to serve the roulade, slice it and arrange it on a platter garnished with the reserved spinach leaves.

# Aubergine and Pepper Relish

Serves 8
Working (and total) time: about 45 minutes

Calories **15**
Protein **0g**
Cholesterol **0mg**
Total fat **1g**
Saturated fat **0g**
Sodium **14mg**

| | | |
|---|---|---|
| 2 | sweet red peppers | 2 |
| 1 tsp | safflower oil | 1 tsp |
| 250 g | aubergine, cut into 5 cm (2 inch) julienne | 8 oz |
| 125 g | celery, finely chopped | 4 oz |
| ¼ tsp | celery seeds | ¼ tsp |
| ¼ tsp | ground coriander | ¼ tsp |
| ⅛ tsp | cayenne pepper | ⅛ tsp |
| 2 tbsp | cider vinegar | 2 tbsp |

Roast the peppers under a preheated grill, turning them with tongs as they blister, until their skins are blackened all over — about 15 minutes. Transfer the peppers to a bowl and cover it with plastic film; the trapped steam will loosen the peppers' skins. When the peppers are cool enough to handle, skin, seed and derib them. Cut the peppers into julienne and set them aside.

Heat the oil in a large, non-stick frying pan over medium-high heat. Add the aubergine and celery, cooking them until they are soft and lightly browned — about 5 minutes. Take the pan off the heat and stir in the red pepper julienne, celery seeds, coriander, cayenne pepper and vinegar. Let the relish cool completely and spoon it into a serving dish. Serve the relish at room temperature.

# Green Beans with Garlic and Bacon

Serves 8
Working time: about 30 minutes
Total time: about 45 minutes

Calories **65**
Protein **4g**
Cholesterol **7mg**
Total fat **2g**
Saturated fat **1g**
Sodium **120mg**

| | | |
|---|---|---|
| 1 tsp | safflower oil | 1 tsp |
| 750 g | fresh French beans, trimmed and cut into 2.5 cm (1 inch) pieces | 1½ lb |
| 2 tbsp | finely chopped garlic | 2 tbsp |
| 1 tbsp | grated lemon rind | 1 tbsp |
| 35 cl | unsalted chicken stock (recipe, page 138) | 12 fl oz |
| 60 g | mild back bacon or lean ham, finely chopped | 2 oz |
| | freshly ground black pepper | |
| 1 | large ripe tomato, cored and cut into wedges | 1 |

Heat the oil in a large non-stick frying pan over medium heat. Add the French beans, garlic and lemon rind and cook them for 1 minute. Pour in the chicken stock, bring the liquid to the boil, and cook the mixture, stirring frequently, until most of the stock has evaporated and the beans are tender — about 5 minutes.

Remove the pan from the heat and stir in the bacon

or ham and some freshly ground pepper. Transfer the beans to a serving plate and let them cool. Arrange the tomato wedges round the beans. Serve the dish at room temperature or chilled.

# Orange-Walnut Coffee Cake

Serves 8
Working time: about 30 minutes
Total time: about 1 hour

Calories **230**
Protein **3g**
Cholesterol **0mg**
Total fat **9g**
Saturated fat **0g**
Sodium **170mg**

| | | |
|---|---|---|
| ¼ litre | fresh orange juice | 8 fl oz |
| 90 g | dark brown sugar | 3 oz |
| 4 tbsp | safflower oil | 4 tbsp |
| 2 | oranges, grated rind only | 2 |
| 150 g | plain flour | 5 oz |
| 1 tsp | baking powder | 1 tsp |
| 1 tsp | bicarbonate of soda | 1 tsp |
| 60 g | rolled oats | 2 oz |
| 1 | egg white | 1 |
| **Streusel topping** | | |
| ½ tsp | cinnamon | ½ tsp |
| 1 tsp | pure vanilla extract | 1 tsp |
| 2 tbsp | chopped walnuts | 2 tbsp |
| 2 tbsp | rolled oats | 2 tbsp |

Preheat the oven to 180°C (350°F or Mark 4). Lightly grease a 22 by 10 cm (9 by 4 inch) loaf tin.

Combine the orange juice, brown sugar, oil and orange rind in a large saucepan and bring the mixture to the boil, stirring constantly. Remove the pan from the heat and let the syrup cool while you prepare the remaining ingredients.

Combine the streusel ingredients in a small bowl; set the bowl aside. Sift the plain flour, baking powder ▶

and bicarbonate of soda together into a bowl. Put the rolled oats in a food processor or a blender and process them into a powder — about 30 seconds. Stir the ground oats into the flour mixture.

When the orange juice syrup is cool, whisk in the egg white. Stir in the flour mixture, until the ingredients are just blended; do not overmix. Pour half of the batter into the prepared tin and then sprinkle half of the streusel mixture over the batter. Pour the remaining streusel over the top.

Bake the coffee cake until a skewer inserted into the centre comes out clean — 25 to 30 minutes. Let the cake cool in the pan for 15 minutes, then turn it out on to a rack to cool completely before slicing it. Serve the cake slices topped with fresh peach compote.

## Fresh Peach Compote

Serves 8
Working time: about 20 minutes
Total time: about 1 hour and 20 minutes
(includes chilling)

Calories **65**
Protein **1g**
Cholesterol **0mg**
Total fat **0g**
Saturated fat **0g**
Sodium **0mg**

| | | |
|---|---|---|
| 750 g | ripe peaches, peeled, stoned and thinly sliced | 1½ lb |
| 3 tbsp | sugar | 3 tbsp |
| 3 tbsp | Cointreau or other orange-flavoured liqueur | 3 tbsp |
| 6 tbsp | fresh orange juice | 6 tbsp |

Combine the sugar, liqueur and orange juice in a small saucepan. Bring the mixture to the boil over medium heat and cook it for 1 minute. Put the peaches into a bowl, pour in the syrup, and stir well. Refrigerate the compote until it is well chilled — about 1 hour.

## Raspberry Iced Tea

Serves 8
Working time: about 20 minutes
Total time: about 1 hour and 20 minutes
(includes chilling)

Calories **45**
Protein **1g**
Cholesterol **0mg**
Total fat **0g**
Saturated fat **0g**
Sodium **1mg**

| | | |
|---|---|---|
| 175 to 250 g | fresh or frozen raspberries | 6 to 8 oz |
| 1 | orange, pared rind and juice | 1 |
| 3 tbsp | honey | 3 tbsp |
| 2 | jasmine tea bags, or 1½ tbsp loose jasmine tea | 2 |
| 1 | lemon, cut into eight slices, for garnish | 1 |

Thaw frozen raspberries, if using. Purée the raspberries in a blender or food processor. Use a wooden spoon to rub the purée through a fine sieve set over a bowl.

Put the orange rind, orange juice, honey and 1.5 litres (2½ pints) of water into a saucepan. Bring the liquid to the boil and add the tea. Remove the saucepan from the heat and let the tea steep for 3 minutes. Strain the tea into the purée, stir the mixture, then chill it.

Serve the drink garnished with the lemon slices.

Most of the dishes can be prepared ahead. Chill the potatoes for the lefse dough. Make the biscuit dough and the berry soup. Prepare the beetroot and cabbage salad and the mackerel salad; salt the cucumbers for the cucumber salad. Bake the biscuits and place them in an airtight container. Refrigerate everything else overnight, covered. Make the lefse and store them in the refrigerator or freezer *(Editor's note, page 90)*.

Just before the brunch, make the green sauce, decorate the fish salad, and heat the lefse.

# Chilled Berry Soup

Serves 8
Working time: about 30 minutes
Total time: about 2 hours and 30 minutes
(includes chilling)

Calories **140**
Protein **2g**
Cholesterol **1mg**
Total fat **1g**
Saturated fat **0g**
Sodium **40mg**

| | | |
|---|---|---|
| 500 g | fresh or frozen raspberries, thawed | 1 lb |
| 600 g | fresh or frozen blueberries, thawed | 1 ¼ lb |
| ¼ litre | dry sherry | 8 fl oz |
| ¼ litre | cranberry juice | 8 fl oz |
| 2 tsp | cider vinegar, raspberry vinegar or blueberry vinegar | 2 tsp |
| 2 tbsp | sugar | 2 tbsp |
| ¼ litre | buttermilk | 8 fl oz |

Set aside 24 raspberries to use as a garnish for the soup. Put the remaining raspberries, the blueberries, sherry, cranberry juice, vinegar and sugar into a non-reactive saucepan and bring the mixture to the boil. Reduce the heat and simmer the mixture for 5 minutes.

Purée the soup in three or four batches in a blender or a food processor. After each batch is puréed, strain it through a fine sieve into a bowl. Cover the soup with plastic film and refrigerate it for at least 2 hours.

To serve, divide the soup between eight bowls and garnish each serving with three of the reserved raspberries and some of the buttermilk. Pass the remaining buttermilk separately in a jug for each diner to add to the soup as desired.

---

*Cool Scandinavian flavours of three salads — beetroot and cabbage, sliced cucumber, and creamy mackerel and potato — accompany a curry-flavoured potato bread called lefse, served with yogurt cheese. A buttermilk-topped berry soup and spice biscuits round out the meal.*

# Curried Potato Lefse

Makes 16 lefse
Working time: about 1 hour and 30 minutes
Total time: about 5 hours and 45 minutes
(includes chilling)

Per lefse:
Calories **130**
Protein **2g**
Cholesterol **0mg**
Total fat **3g**
Saturated fat **0g**
Sodium **4mg**

| | | |
|---|---|---|
| 1 kg | medium-sized potatoes, peeled and quartered | 2 lb |
| 4 tbsp | safflower oil | 4 tbsp |
| 4 tbsp | skimmed milk | 4 tbsp |
| 1 tsp | curry powder | 1 tsp |
| 325 g | plain flour | 11 oz |

Bring 2 litres (3½ pints) of water to the boil in a large saucepan. Add the potatoes, then reduce the heat, and simmer them until they are tender — about 10 minutes. Drain the potatoes thoroughly. Work the potatoes through a food mill, a sieve or a ricer set over a bowl. Allow the potatoes to cool to room temperature, then cover the bowl with plastic film and refrigerate the potatoes until they are very cold — at least 4 hours.

Add the oil, milk and curry powder to the cold potatoes. Stir the mixture until it is smooth. Add the flour, about 70 g (2½ oz) at a time, kneading the mixture against the sides of the bowl with the heel of your hand after each addition. The dough should be firm but not dry.

Divide the dough into 16 pieces. Preheat an electric skillet to 200°C (400°F) or heat a large, non-stick frying pan (box, page 55) over medium-high heat.

Lightly flour a work surface; use only enough flour to prevent sticking — too much will make the lefse brittle. Use a rolling pin to roll one piece of the dough into a round no more than 3 mm (⅛ inch) thick; the lefse should be as thin as possible. Roll out the remaining pieces of dough in the same manner, stacking the rounds one on top of another.

Put one of the rounds on the preheated skillet and cook it until the underside is flecked with brown speckles — about 1 minute. Turn the lefse over and brown the other side.

Transfer the cooked lefse to a clean tea towel or cloth spread flat on a work surface and fold the lefse into quarters. Cover the folded lefse with another towel or cloth. Continue to cook the remaining rounds in the same manner, folding and covering each lefse as it is cooked. When the lefse have cooled to room temperature, remove them from the towels and wrap them tightly in plastic film until you are ready to serve.

Serve the lefse with dill and chive spread (recipe, page 51).

---

EDITOR'S NOTE: The lefse can be prepared a day in advance and refrigerated. Divide the folded lefse into groups of four and wrap them in aluminium foil. Reheat the wrapped lefse in a preheated 100°C (200°F or Mark ¼) oven for about 10 minutes. The wrapped lefse can also be kept in the freezer for up to one month; thaw them and reheat them as described.

# Mackerel and Red Potato Salad

Serves 8
Working time: about 1 hour and 15 minutes
Total time: about 3 hours and 15 minutes
(includes chilling)

Calories **170**
Protein **11g**
Cholesterol **40mg**
Total fat **7g**
Saturated fat **2g**
Sodium **165mg**

| | | |
|---|---|---|
| 500 g | mackerel or trout fillets, skinned and cut into 2.5 cm (1 inch) pieces | 1 lb |
| 350 g | red potatoes, scrubbed and cut into 1 cm (½ inch) cubes | 12 oz |
| 1 | red apple, cored and chopped | 1 |
| 1 | small onion, thinly sliced | 1 |
| 2 tsp | capers, rinsed and chopped | 2 tsp |
| 6 tbsp | cider vinegar | 6 tbsp |
| 2 tsp | safflower oil | 2 tsp |
| 1 tbsp | caster sugar | 1 tbsp |
| | freshly ground black pepper | |
| 4 tbsp | plain low-fat yogurt | 4 tbsp |
| 30 g | radishes, sliced | 1 oz |
| 1 | carrot, thinly sliced | 1 |
| 4 tbsp | chopped fresh parsley | 4 tbsp |
| 2 tbsp | finely cut chives | 2 tbsp |

Pour enough water into a large shallow pan to fill it 5 cm (2 inches) deep. Bring the water to a simmer, add the mackerel or trout, and poach them over medium-low heat until the flesh is opaque and firm to the touch — about 2 minutes. Remove the fish pieces from the water with a slotted spoon and arrange them in a single layer in the bottom of a deep serving dish.

Pour enough water into a large saucepan to fill it about 2.5 cm (1 inch) deep. Set a vegetable steamer in the pan and put the potatoes into it. Cover the pan and bring the water to the boil. Steam the potatoes until they are tender — about 10 minutes.

In a bowl, toss the potatoes with the apple, onion and capers. Spread the mixture over the mackerel.

Whisk together the vinegar, oil, sugar and some pepper; pour this dressing over the potatoes. Cover the dish and refrigerate it for at least 2 hours. (The salad can be refrigerated for as long as overnight.)

Just before serving, spread the yogurt in a thin layer over the salad. Arrange the radish slices, carrot slices, parsley and chives on top, and serve.

## Grated Beetroot and Red Cabbage Salad

Serves 8
Working time: about 30 minutes
Total time: about 1 hour and 40 minutes
(includes chilling)

Calories **30**
Protein **1g**
Cholesterol **0mg**
Total fat **0g**
Saturated fat **0g**
Sodium **85mg**

| | | |
|---|---|---|
| 350 g | beetroots, scrubbed and trimmed, 5 cm (2 inches) of stem left on each beetroot | 12 oz |
| 250 g | red cabbage, thinly sliced | 8 oz |
| 4 tbsp | unsweetened apple juice | 4 tbsp |
| 12.5 cl | cranberry sauce | 4 fl oz |
| 4 tbsp | cider vinegar | 4 tbsp |
| ¼ tsp | salt | ¼ tsp |
| 1 tsp | caraway seeds | 1 tsp |

Put the beetroots into a saucepan with enough water to cover them by 7.5 cm (3 inches). Bring the water to the boil over high heat, reduce the heat, and simmer the beetroots until they are tender — about 20 minutes. Remove the beetroots from the water and set them aside to cool.

While the beetroots are cooking, combine the cabbage, apple juice, cranberry juice, vinegar and salt in a nonreactive saucepan. Bring the mixture to the boil over high heat, reduce the heat, and simmer the cabbage for 5 minutes. Transfer the cabbage mixture to a large bowl.

When the beetroots are cool enough to handle, peel and grate them, using the grater's coarsest side. Toss the beetroots with the cabbage and the caraway seeds; refrigerate the salad, covered, for at least 1 hour.

EDITOR'S NOTE: *If you wish, this salad can be made up to two days in advance.*

## Cucumber Salad with Creamy Green Sauce

Serves 8
Working time: about 30 minutes
Total time: about 7 hours (includes chilling)

Calories **20**
Protein **1g**
Cholesterol **2mg**
Total fat **1g**
Saturated fat **0g**
Sodium **280mg**

| | | |
|---|---|---|
| 2 | cucumbers, peeled and thinly sliced | 2 |
| 1 tsp | salt | 1 tsp |
| | **Creamy green sauce** | |
| 1 | bunch watercress, stemmed, washed and dried | 1 |
| 1 | small spring onion, trimmed and coarsely chopped | 1 |
| 60 g | low-fat ricotta cheese | 2 oz |
| 1 tbsp | fresh lemon juice | 1 tbsp |
| 1 tsp | caster sugar | 1 tsp |

Toss the cucumber slices with the salt in a bowl. Cover the bowl and refrigerate it for at least 6 hours.

Rinse the cucumber slices in a colander under cold running water. Drain them thoroughly and transfer them to a salad bowl.

To make the green sauce, purée the watercress, spring onion, cheese, lemon juice and sugar in a blender or a food processor. Pour the sauce over the cucumber slices and toss to mix them well. Refrigerate the salad for at least 30 minutes before serving.

## Half-Moon Spice Biscuits

Makes 24 biscuits
Working time: about 30 minutes
Total time: about 1 hour

*Per biscuit:*
Calories **20**
Protein **0g**
Cholesterol **1mg**
Total fat **1g**
Saturated fat **0g**
Sodium **6mg**

| | | |
|---|---|---|
| 2 tbsp | golden syrup | 2 tbsp |
| 1 tbsp | light or dark brown sugar | 1 tbsp |
| 15 g | unsalted butter, softened | ½ oz |
| 75 g | plain flour, sifted | 2½ oz |
| ¼ tsp | ground cloves | ¼ tsp |
| ½ tsp | grated lemon rind | ½ tsp |
| 1 | egg white, beaten | 1 |
| 1 tbsp | slivered almonds | 1 tbsp |

Put the golden syrup, sugar and butter into a small bowl. Using a wooden spoon, cream the ingredients together. Add the flour, cloves and rind and mix until the dry ingredients are incorporated. Wrap the dough in plastic film and refrigerate it for 30 minutes.

Preheat the oven to 200°C (400°F or Mark 6). Lightly oil a baking sheet or line it with parchment paper.

Place the chilled dough on a lightly floured surface and roll it about 3 mm (⅛ inch) thick. Using a biscuit cutter with a 5 cm (2 inch) diameter, cut the dough into rounds. Gather the scraps into a ball, then roll out the dough, and cut more rounds; there should be 12 in all. Brush the rounds with egg white, then cut them in half; press an almond sliver on to each half. Transfer the biscuits to the baking sheet. Bake the biscuits until they have lightened slightly in colour — 5 to 7 minutes. Transfer the biscuits to a rack to cool. Store the cooled biscuits in an airtight container.

To avoid a last-minute rush, make the oat and onion bread and the buttermilk fruit tea bread the day before you plan to serve this British brunch. On the day of the brunch, first make the vegetable salad and leave it to chill. Prepare the citrus tea punch and the maple-lime dip. One and a half hours before serving time, make the kedgeree, and while it is cooking prepare the fresh fruits for the kebabs.

# Fresh Fruit Kebabs with Maple-Lime Dip

Serves 8
Working (and total) time: about 35 minutes

Calories **120**
Protein **6g**
Cholesterol **0mg**
Total fat **2g**
Saturated fat **1g**
Sodium **120mg**

| | | |
|---|---|---|
| 1 | pineapple, halved lengthwise | 1 |
| 24 | melon balls, scooped from one small melon | 24 |
| 24 | strawberries, hulled | 24 |
| 2 | peaches, each peeled, stoned and cut into 12 wedges | 2 |
| 2 | nectarines, each stoned and cut into 12 wedges | 2 |
| 24 | seedless green grapes | 24 |
| 2 | bananas, each cut into 12 rounds | 2 |
| 2 | limes, juice only | 2 |
| **Maple-lime dip** | | |
| 30 cl | fromage frais | ½ pint |
| 2 tbsp | pure maple syrup | 2 tbsp |
| ½ | lime, grated rind only | ½ |

Make the dip by mixing together the *fromage frais*, maple syrup and grated lime rind. Put it into a small serving bowl and set aside.

Hollow out one pineapple half. Cut the flesh into ▶

*The central feature of this British brunch is a spicy haddock kedgeree. It is preceded by chunks of fresh fruit served with a maple-lime dip and accompanied by a salad with a mint dressing. Two kinds of loaf — an oat bread and a buttermilk tea bread — and a citrus tea punch complete the meal.*

chunks and reserve the shell. Keep the other half of the pineapple for another use. In another bowl, mix the pineapple chunks, melon balls, strawberries, peaches, nectarines, grapes and bananas together with the lime juice to prevent discoloration.

Fill the hollowed pineapple shell with the assorted fruits. Serve the filled pineapple on a large dish together with kebab sticks and the bowl of dip, so that guests can select, skewer and dip the fruits of their choice.

# Kedgeree

Serves 8
Working time: about 30 minutes
Total time: about 1 hour and 30 minutes

Calories **30**
Protein **18g**
Cholesterol **90mg**
Total fat **3g**
Saturated fat **1g**
Sodium **250mg**

| | | |
|---|---|---|
| 500 g | fresh haddock fillet | 1 lb |
| 125 g | smoked haddock fillet | 4 oz |
| 1 tbsp | safflower oil | 1 tbsp |
| 1 | onion, thinly sliced | 1 |
| 2 tsp | mild chili powder | 2 tsp |
| 1 tsp | turmeric | 1 tsp |
| 1 tsp | ground ginger | 1 tsp |
| ½ tsp | ground coriander | ½ tsp |
| ½ tsp | ground cumin | ½ tsp |
| ¼ tsp | mixed spice | ¼ tsp |
| ½ tsp | salt | ½ tsp |
| | freshly ground black pepper | |
| 500 g | long-grain rice | 1 lb |
| 2 | hard-boiled eggs, quartered | 2 |
| | chopped fresh chives or parsley, for garnish | |

Put the fresh haddock into a large saucepan and add water to cover. Bring the water to a simmer and poach the fish for 5 minutes. Add the smoked haddock and continue poaching for 5 to 10 minutes or until both fish are cooked and flake easily when tested with a fork.

Drain the fish, reserving the cooking liquid. When the fish are cool enough to handle, flake them, discarding all skin and bones. Set the flaked fish aside and keep it warm.

Strain the cooking liquid and measure it; you will need 1.25 litres (2 pints); if necessary, add a little water.

Heat the oil in a large fireproof casserole or saucepan. Add the onion and cook gently, covered, for about 7 minutes or until softened. If necessary, add a few spoonfuls of the reserved cooking liquid to prevent the onion sticking and burning.

Stir in all the spices, the salt, some pepper and 2 to 3 more spoonfuls of the cooking liquid. Add the rice and stir until it is coated with the spice mixture. Add the remaining liquid and bring to the boil. Stir once, then cover and cook over very low heat for about 20 minutes or until the rice is cooked and tender and all the liquid has been absorbed.

Fluff the rice up with a fork. Gently fold in the flaked fish. Turn the mixture into a warmed serving dish. Garnish with the egg quarters and sprinkle with chopped chives or parsley. Serve hot.

# Vegetable Salad with Mint Vinaigrette

Serves 8
Working time: about 30 minutes
Total time: about 2 hours and 30 minutes

Calories **180**
Protein **1g**
Cholesterol **0mg**
Total fat **18g**
Saturated fat **3g**
Sodium **110mg**

| | | |
|---|---|---|
| 1 | cauliflower, thick stalks trimmed, broken into small florets | 1 |
| ½ | cucumber, julienned | ½ |
| 250 g | daikon radish (mooli), peeled and julienned | 8 oz |
| 1 | sweet red pepper, seeded, deribbed and julienned | 1 |
| 250 g | carrots, julienned | 8 oz |
| 2 | large sticks celery, thinly sliced | 2 |
| 1 | bunch spring onions, chopped | 1 |
| 2 to 3 tbsp | chopped fresh mint | 2 to 3 tbsp |
| **Mint vinaigrette** | | |
| 8 tbsp | virgin olive oil | 8 tbsp |
| 2 tbsp | lemon juice | 2 tbsp |
| 1 tbsp | red wine vinegar | 1 tbsp |
| ½ tsp | Dijon mustard | ½ tsp |
| ½ tsp | caster sugar | ½ tsp |
| ½ tsp | salt | ½ tsp |
| | freshly ground black pepper | |

Bring a large pan of water to the boil. Drop in the cauliflower florets and blanch them for 4 minutes. Drain and refresh them under cold running water. Drain them again and pat them dry with paper towels.

To make the vinaigrette, combine the oil, lemon juice, vinegar, mustard, sugar, salt and some pepper in a large mixing bowl, whisking well to blend. Toss the cauliflower florets in the dressing to coat them. Then add the cucumber, radish, pepper, carrot, celery and spring onions and mix well. Cover the salad and chill it for at least 2 hours before serving.

# Oat and Onion Bread

Serves 8
Working time: about 50 minutes
Total time: about 4 hours and 30 minutes

Calories **395**
Protein **11g**
Cholesterol **0mg**
Total fat **7g**
Saturated fat **1g**
Sodium **170mg**

| | | |
|---|---|---|
| 250 g | porridge oats | 8 oz |
| 17.5 cl | semi-skimmed milk | 6 fl oz |
| ½ tsp | caster sugar | ½ tsp |
| 1 tbsp | dried yeast | 1 tbsp |
| 500 g | strong plain flour | 1 lb |

| 1 tsp | salt | 1 tsp |
|---|---|---|
| 2 tsp | dry mustard | 2 tsp |
| 2 tbsp | safflower oil | 2 tbsp |
| 1 | large onion, finely chopped | 1 |

Put the oats, 30 cl (½ pint) of water and 15 cl (¼ pint) of the milk in a bowl. Stir the mixture, then set it aside for 1 hour to allow the oats to absorb the liquid.

Warm 5 cl (2 fl oz) of water to blood heat and put it in a small bowl. Stir in the sugar until dissolved, then sprinkle over the yeast and whisk briefly. Cover the bowl and leave it in a warm place until the yeast foams, 10 to 15 minutes.

Sift the flour, salt and mustard into a large bowl. Make a well in the centre and add the oat mixture and the yeast liquid. Mix to a soft and sticky dough.

Turn out the dough on to a well-floured surface and knead it for about 10 minutes or until it is smooth and elastic; sprinkle more flour on the work surface, if necessary. Shape the dough into a ball.

Put 2 teaspoons of the oil in a clean mixing bowl. Place the dough in the bowl and turn to coat it with oil on all sides. Cover the dough and leave it to rise in a warm place for 1½ to 2 hours, or until doubled in bulk.

Meanwhile, heat the remaining oil in a frying pan over medium-high heat and add the onion. Reduce the heat, cover the pan and cook the onion gently until it is very soft and beginning to brown — about 10 minutes. Drain the onion well on paper towels.

Turn out the risen dough on to a lightly floured surface, knock it back and knead it until smooth and elastic again. Knead in the onion until evenly distributed. Divide the dough in half and shape each piece into a round loaf. Place the loaves on a floured baking sheet, leaving enough room for spreading. Cover and leave to prove in a warm place for about 45 minutes.

Preheat the oven to 220°C (425°F or Mark 7).

Uncover the dough and brush each loaf with the rest of the milk. Bake for 30 to 35 minutes or until the loaves are browned and sound hollow when rapped on the base with your knuckles. Transfer the loaves to a wire rack to cool.

# Buttermilk Fruit Tea Bread

Serves 8
Working time: about 20 minutes
Total time: about 1 hour and 10 minutes

Calories **200**
Protein **5g**
Cholesterol **30mg**
Total fat **4g**
Saturated fat **1g**
Sodium **230mg**

| 250 g | plain flour | 8 oz |
|---|---|---|
| 1 tsp | bicarbonate of soda | 1 tsp |
| 1 tsp | ground coriander | 1 tsp |
| ¼ tsp | salt | ¼ tsp |
| 30 g | polyunsaturated margarine | 1 oz |
| 60 g | quark | 2 oz |
| 60 g | light muscovado sugar | 2 oz |
| 1 | egg, beaten | 1 |
| 15 cl | buttermilk | ¼ pint |
| 45 g | raisins | 1½ oz |
| 45 g | sultanas | 1½ oz |

Preheat the oven to 180°C (350°F or Mark 4).

Sift the flour, soda, coriander and salt into a bowl. In another bowl, beat all but 1 teaspoon of the margarine and quark with the sugar until smooth and creamy. Beat in the egg. Add the flour mixture alternately with the buttermilk, beating well between each addition. Stir in the raisins and sultanas.

Grease a 500 g (1 lb) loaf tin with the reserved margarine and coat with flour, shaking out the excess. Spoon the cake mixture into the tin and spread it out so that there is a slight depression in the centre (this will prevent the tea bread rising too high in the centre).

Bake for 50 minutes to 1 hour, or until the bread has risen and browned — a skewer inserted into the centre should come out clean. Leave the bread to cool in the tin for 10 minutes, then turn it out on to a wire rack to cool completely.

# Citrus Tea Punch

Serves 8
Working time: about 20 minutes
Total time: about 1 hour and 30 minutes

Calories **155**
Protein **0g**
Cholesterol **0mg**
Total fat **0g**
Saturated fat **0g**
Sodium **0mg**

| 4 tsp | Indian tea leaves | 4 tsp |
|---|---|---|
| 1 | cinnamon stick | 1 |
| 4 | cloves | 4 |
| 3 | allspice berries | 3 |
| 1 | slice fresh ginger root | 1 |
| 90 g | caster sugar | 3 oz |
| 60 cl | fresh orange juice | 1 pint |
| 15 cl | fresh lemon juice | ¼ pint |
| 30 cl | light rum, vodka or brandy | ½ pint |
| | soda or mineral water (optional) | |
| | lime and orange slices | |

Put the tea leaves, cinnamon, cloves, allspice and ginger in a bowl or large jug and pour on 1 litre (1¾ pints) of boiling water. Cover the infusion and leave it for 10 minutes.

Strain the spiced tea into a second clean bowl or jug, add the sugar and stir until it dissolves. Add the orange and lemon juice. Allow the mixture to cool, then put the bowl into the refrigerator and leave it for at least 1 hour to chill well.

When the time comes to serve the punch, stir in the rum, vodka or brandy. Serve the punch in a bowl, with soda or mineral water added to taste, garnished with lime and orange slices.

EDITOR'S NOTE: *The alcohol may be omitted.*

---

### CHINESE BRUNCH

*Rice Congee*
*Fried Chinese Turnip Cakes*
*Beef Pot Stickers with Soy Dipping Sauce*
*Steamed Buns Filled with Sweet Red Bean Paste*
*Almond Milk with Apricots*

---

Simplify the preparation of this brunch by making the congee, buns, almond jelly and the sauce for the pot stickers the day before; refrigerate them overnight. Cook the mixture for the turnip cakes in advance and leave it in the loaf dish. Form the pot stickers and cover them with a damp towel and plastic film. Put the steamed buns into an airtight bag.

On the day of the brunch, reheat the congee and prepare its garnishes; if the congee has thickened, add a little stock or water to thin it. Cook the pot stickers and, while they simmer, slice and fry the turnip cakes. The buns need only to be steamed briefly to reheat them. To serve the jelly, simply cut it into squares.

# Rice Congee

CONGEE IS A CHINESE PORRIDGE THAT CAN BE FLAVOURED
WITH A VARIETY OF INGREDIENTS, BOTH SWEET AND SAVOURY.

Serves 8
Working time: about 30 minutes
Total time: about 1 hour

Calories **165**
Protein **10g**
Cholesterol **20mg**
Total fat **1g**
Saturated fat **0g**
Sodium **130mg**

| | | |
|---|---|---|
| 135 g | long-grain rice | 4½ oz |
| 1 litre | unsalted brown or chicken stock (recipes, page 138) | 1¾ pints |
| 1 tbsp | safflower oil | 1 tbsp |
| 6 | garlic cloves, finely chopped | 6 |
| 60 g | fresh ginger root, julienned | 2 oz |
| 125 g | bean sprouts | 4 oz |
| 45 g | fresh coriander leaves | 1½ oz |
| 1 | lime, cut into 16 wedges | 1 |
| 2 tbsp | sugar | 2 tbsp |
| 1 tsp | fish sauce or low-sodium soy sauce | 1 tsp |
| 1 tsp | salt | 1 tsp |
| | freshly ground black pepper | |
| 250 g | beef fillet, trimmed of fat and cut into thin strips | 8 oz |
| 3 | spring onions, trimmed and cut into 1 cm (½ inch) lengths | 3 |

Put the rice, stock and 1 litre (1¾ pints) of water into a large saucepan; bring the liquid to the boil. Stir the mixture, then reduce the heat to medium, and simmer

---

*This Chinese brunch begins with a bowl of rice soup, called congee, and, on the tray, a selection of garnishes. Beef pot stickers with soy dipping sauce, steamed buns filled with bean paste, and fried turnip cakes follow. Squares of almond milk jelly provide the refreshing dessert.*

the rice, uncovered, until it is very soft and begins to break apart — about 1 hour.

While the rice is cooking, heat the safflower oil in a small frying pan over medium-low heat. Add the garlic and cook it, stirring often, until it is crisp and brown — 4 to 5 minutes. Transfer the garlic to a paper towel and let it drain. Put the garlic, ginger, bean sprouts, coriander and lime wedges into small serving bowls, and set them aside.

About 5 minutes before serving, stir the sugar, fish sauce or soy sauce, salt and some pepper into the hot soup. Add the beef strips and spring onions, and bring the liquid to the boil. Reduce the heat to medium and simmer the soup until the beef is just cooked — about 3 minutes.

Ladle the soup into individual bowls. Pass the garnishes separately inviting the diners to season their own soup with them.

# Fried Chinese Turnip Cakes

Serves 8
Working time: about 20 minutes
Total time: about 1 hour and 20 minutes

Calories **60**
Protein **2g**
Cholesterol **0mg**
Total fat **1g**
Saturated fat **0g**
Sodium **90mg**

| | | |
|---|---|---|
| 750 g | white turnip, or daikon radish, (mooli) peeled and coarsely grated | 1½ lb |
| 12.5 cl | unsalted chicken stock (recipe, page 138) | 4 fl oz |
| 75 g | plain flour | 2½ oz |
| 15 g | dried shrimps, finely chopped | ½ oz |
| ½ | sweet red or green pepper, seeded, deribbed and finely diced | ½ |
| 2 | egg whites, lightly beaten | 2 |
| 2 tsp | rice vinegar or distilled white vinegar | 2 tsp |
| ¼ tsp | salt | ¼ tsp |
| | freshly ground black pepper | |
| 2 tsp | safflower oil | 2 tsp |

Pour enough water into a large saucepan to fill it about 2.5 cm (1 inch) deep. Set a vegetable steamer in the pan and bring the water to the boil. Put the turnip into the steamer, cover the pan and reduce the heat to medium low. Steam the turnip until it is very tender — about 15 minutes. While the turnip is cooking, blend the chicken stock and flour in a 2 litre (3½ pint) saucepan to form a smooth paste.

Drain the turnip in a sieve, pressing it with the back of a wooden spoon to get rid of any excess water. Add the turnip to the flour paste and cook the mixture over low heat, stirring constantly for 3 minutes.

Remove the pan from the heat and stir in the dried shrimps, red or green pepper, egg whites, vinegar, salt, and one or two grindings of black pepper. Spoon the mixture into a lightly oiled 10 by 20 cm (4 by 8 inch) glass or enamelled loaf dish, smooth the top with the back ►

of a spoon and cover the pan lightly with plastic film.

Place the loaf dish in a pan large enough to hold it and pour in 1 cm (½ inch) of water. Bring the water to the boil. Cover the pan, reduce the heat to medium low, and poach the loaf until it is firm to the touch — about 40 minutes. Remove the loaf dish from the pan and allow the loaf to cool completely. If you wish, it may be chilled overnight.

Loosen the loaf from the sides of the dish with a knife, then turn it out on to a cutting board. Cut the loaf into 5 mm (¼ inch) slices.

Brush a large, non-stick frying pan with 1 teaspoon of the oil, then set the pan over medium-high heat. Add half of the turnip cake slices and sauté them, turning them once, until they are brown on both sides. Transfer the slices to a heated platter. Brush the pan with the remaining oil and brown the remaining slices in the same manner.

EDITOR'S NOTE: *Dried shrimps are available in Asian shops.*

# Beef Pot Stickers with Soy Dipping Sauce

Serves 8
Working time: about 1 hour
Total time: about 1 hour and 30 minutes

Calories **60**
Protein **7g**
Cholesterol **7mg**
Total fat **1g**
Saturated fat **0g**
Sodium **130mg**

| | | |
|---|---|---|
| 250 g | Chinese cabbage or green cabbage, cut into fine shreds | 8 oz |
| 125 g | beef topside, minced | 4 oz |
| 15 g | fresh water chestnuts (about five), peeled and chopped, or canned water chestnuts, rinsed, drained and chopped | ½ oz |
| 1 | spring onion, trimmed and finely chopped | 1 |
| 1 tbsp | rice wine or dry sherry | 1 tbsp |
| 1 tsp | low-sodium soy sauce or shoyu | 1 tsp |
| ⅛ tsp | white pepper | ⅛ tsp |
| 1 tsp | cornflour | 1 tsp |
| 24 | wonton wrappers, trimmed into circles, or 24 gyoza wrappers (plus two or three extra wrappers to use if others tear) | 24 |
| 1 tsp | safflower oil | 1 tsp |
| **Soy dipping sauce** | | |
| 12.5 cl | unsalted chicken or brown stock (recipes, page 138) | 4 fl oz |
| 3 tbsp | rice vinegar or distilled white vinegar | 3 tbsp |
| 1 tbsp | low-sodium soy sauce or shoyu | 1 tbsp |
| 1 tbsp | trimmed, julienned spring onions | 1 tbsp |
| 1 tbsp | finely julienned carrot | 1 tbsp |
| 1 tsp | caster sugar | 1 tsp |

Put all of the ingredients for the soy dipping sauce into a small, decorative bowl and stir them until the sugar is dissolved. Set the bowl aside.

Put the shredded cabbage into a colander and set it in the sink or over a large bowl. Pour about 1 litre (1¾ pints) of boiling water over the cabbage to blanch it. Press out any excess water with the back of a wooden spoon.

To prepare the filling, put the beef into a large bowl and add the blanched cabbage, water chestnuts, spring onion, wine, soy sauce, pepper and cornflour. Stir the contents of the bowl thoroughly.

To make the dumplings, place a heaped teaspoon of the filling on a wrapper, slightly off centre. Fold the circle into a crescent-shaped dumpling *(page 124)*. Repeat the process with the remaining wrappers, covering the dumplings with a slightly damp cloth as they are completed. (The dumplings can be made ahead of time and kept in the refrigerator, covered, on a lightly floured tray.)

Brush the safflower oil on to the surface of a non-stick frying pan and set the pan over medium-high heat. When the pan is hot, arrange as many of the dumplings as will fit in a single layer in the pan without touching one another; the sealed sides should face up. Reduce the heat to medium and cook the dumplings until they turn golden-brown on the bottom. Add enough cold water to come half way up the sides of the dumplings. Partially cover the pan and simmer the dumplings until almost all of the liquid has evaporated or been absorbed by the dumplings — about 10 minutes. Transfer the dumplings to a serving dish and keep them warm while you cook the remaining dumplings. Serve the dumplings with the soy dipping sauce.

EDITOR'S NOTE: *Wonton and gyoza wrappers are available in Chinese and Japanese shops.*

# Steamed Buns Filled with Sweet Red Bean Paste

THESE BUNS CAN BE PREPARED A DAY IN ADVANCE AND REFRIGERATED, THEN STEAMED FOR ABOUT 5 MINUTES TO REHEAT THEM.

Serves 8
Working time: about 50 minutes
Total time: about 4 hours (includes soaking and cooking time for the beans)

Calories **245**
Protein **8g**
Cholesterol **0mg**
Total fat **4g**
Saturated fat **0g**
Sodium **3mg**

| | | |
|---|---|---|
| 1 tbsp | easy-blend dried yeast | 1 tbsp |
| 2 tsp | sugar | 2 tsp |
| 275 g | plain flour, sifted | 9 oz |
| 2 tbsp | safflower oil | 2 tbsp |
| **Sweet red bean paste** | | |
| 250 g | dried red kidney beans, picked over | 8 oz |
| 6 tbsp | sugar | 6 tbsp |
| 1 tsp | pure vanilla extract | 1 tsp |
| 1 tsp | beetroot juice (optional) | 1 tsp |

To prepare the bean paste, rinse the beans and then place them in a small saucepan with enough water to cover them. Discard any beans that float to the surface. Cover the saucepan, leaving the lid ajar, and slowly bring the liquid to the boil over medium-low heat. Boil the beans for 2 minutes, then turn off the heat and soak the beans, covered, for at least 1 hour.

After the beans have finished soaking, drain them and return them to the pan. Pour in ¾ litre (1¼ pints) of water and bring the beans to the boil. Reduce the heat and simmer them until they begin to split and are very tender — about 1½ hours. Drain the beans, reserving 4 tablespoons of their cooking liquid. Put the beans in a food processor or a blender. Add the sugar, the vanilla extract and the reserved cooking liquid, and purée the mixture.

Transfer the puréed beans to a sieve and, holding it over a small saucepan, force the mixture through the sieve with the back of a spoon. Cook the mixture over low heat, stirring frequently, until all of the excess liquid has evaporated — about 5 minutes. Transfer the bean paste to a bowl, then cover the bowl, and refrigerate the filling until you are ready to fill the buns.

To make the buns, combine the yeast, sugar and flour in a large mixing bowl. Heat 12.5 cl (4 fl oz) of water and the oil in a large saucepan just until they are hot to the touch (43°C/110°F). Stir the hot liquid into the flour mixture with a wooden spoon to combine the ingredients thoroughly. Turn the dough out on to a floured work surface. Knead the dough, adding a few tablespoons of flour if it is too sticky, until the dough is smooth and elastic — 4 to 5 minutes. Transfer the dough to a lightly oiled bowl, turn it once to coat it with the oil, and cover the bowl with a damp towel or plastic film. Place the bowl in a warm, draught-free place and let the dough double in bulk — about 30 minutes.

When the dough has risen, knock it back and then transfer it to a floured work surface. Divide the dough into four pieces; cover three of the pieces with a towel. Roll out one piece of dough into a 5 mm (¼ inch) thick rectangle measuring about 25 by 18 cm (10 by 7 inches).

With a 7.5 cm (3 inch) biscuit cutter, cut out six rounds from the rectangle. Place a half tablespoon of the bean-paste filling in the centre of one round and then gently gather up the edge of the dough around the bean paste; pinch the edge together and twist it closed to form a bun *(page 124)*. Repeat the procedure for the remaining five rounds.

Line two tiers of a bamboo steamer with perforated greaseproof paper. Place the buns, sealed side down, on the paper — about 12 per tier.

Roll out a second piece of dough. Cut out six more rounds and fill them as described above. Position the six new buns on the steamer tray. Continue shaping and filling the remaining dough until you have 24 buns. Cover the trays and place them in a warm draught-free place for 20 minutes.

To steam the buns, set the covered steamer trays in a wok or a pan filled with 2.5 cm (1 inch) of boiling water. Steam the buns until they are firm yet still springy to the touch — about 20 minutes.

Remove the buns from the steamer and, if you like, paint a decorative design on their tops using a small artist's brush dipped in a little beetroot juice.

The buns can be served immediately, or they can be stored in a sealed plastic bag in the refrigerator for a day. Reheat the buns by steaming them, as described above, for 5 to 7 minutes.

EDITOR'S NOTE: *If you do not have a bamboo steamer, you may use a vegetable steamer. Pour enough water into a pan to fill it 2.5 cm (1 inch) deep and set the vegetable steamer in the pan. Cut out 24 small rounds of greaseproof paper and place the buns on the rounds. Arrange as many of the buns as will fit in the steamer without touching each other. Cover the pan and steam the buns as directed in the recipe; repeat the process as many times as necessary to steam the remaining buns. Alternatively, you may set the plate on a bowl in the pan to steam the buns.*

# Almond Milk with Apricots

Serves 8
Working time: about 10 minutes
Total time: about 2 hours and 10 minutes
(includes chilling)

Calories **75**
Protein **4g**
Cholesterol **4mg**
Total fat **1g**
Saturated fat **1g**
Sodium **30mg**

| | | |
|---|---|---|
| 2 | packets powdered gelatine | 2 |
| 35 cl | semi-skimmed milk | 12 fl oz |
| 6 tbsp | sugar | 6 tbsp |
| 1 tbsp | almond extract | 1 tbsp |
| 8 | canned apricot halves, drained, rinsed if packed in syrup, and patted dry | 8 |
| 1 tbsp | flaked almonds (optional) | 1 tbsp |
| 1 tbsp | toasted desiccated coconut (optional) | 1 tbsp |

Pour 12.5 cl (4 fl oz) of cold water into a bowl and sprinkle the gelatine on to the water. While the gelatine softens, bring ¼ litre (8 fl oz) of water to the boil, then pour it into the bowl, stirring to dissolve the gelatine. Add the milk, sugar and almond extract and stir to dissolve the sugar. Pour the mixture into a 20 cm (8 inch) square dish, and distribute the apricot halves in the mixture so that when the dessert is cut into squares each will contain an apricot half. Refrigerate the dessert until it is set — about 2 hours; the dessert may be kept in the refrigerator overnight.

To serve, cut the dessert into squares, place the squares on a serving platter and, if you like, top each with some of the almonds and coconut.

The salsa verde and the tomato salads for this brunch can be prepared a day ahead. If you like, the meat can be sliced and the marinade prepared. Freeze the mixture for the lime drink. Refrigerate everything else.

On the day of the brunch, put the pork into its marinade. Make the strawberry and grapefruit salad and chill it. Shred the lettuce for the tomato salads, then unmould them on to the lettuce. Transfer the pink lime freeze to the refrigerator to soften for about 45 minutes before processing it. About 30 minutes before serving time, make the griddle cakes. Keep the griddle cakes warm while you grill the pork.

# Cornmeal Griddle Cakes

Makes twelve 10 cm (4 inch) cakes
Working (and total) time: about 30 minutes

*Per cake:*
Calories **110**
Protein **4g**
Cholesterol **45mg**
Total fat **2g**
Saturated fat **1g**
Sodium **115mg**

| | | |
|---|---|---:|
| 125 g | cornmeal | 4 oz |
| 1 tsp | sugar | 1 tsp |
| ¼ tsp | salt | ¼ tsp |
| 12.5 cl | semi-skimmed milk | 4 fl oz |
| 1 | egg, lightly beaten | 1 |

Combine the cornmeal, sugar and salt in a bowl. Pour in ¼ litre (8 fl oz) of boiling water all at once and stir until the ingredients are all well blended. Let the mixture stand for 2 minutes.

In a small bowl, whisk together the milk and egg. Pour this mixture into the bowl containing the cornmeal mixture and stir the batter until it is smooth.

Heat a large, non-stick griddle or frying pan *(box, page 55)* over medium-high heat until a few drops of cold water dance when sprinkled on the surface. Drop the batter, 2 tablespoons at a time, on to the hot surface, then use the back of the spoon to spread the batter into 10 cm (4 inch) rounds. Cook the griddle cakes until the surface is covered with bubbles and the underside is browned — about 2 minutes. Turn the cakes over and cook them until the other sides are ▶

---

*Golden cornmeal griddle cakes are served with grilled pork loin and a bowl of zesty salsa verde. Tomato salads on lettuce and a tomato-lime drink accompany the meal. For dessert, strawberries are paired with grapefruit segments.*

browned— about 1 minute more.

Transfer the griddle cakes to a serving plate and keep them warm while you cook the remaining batter. Serve the griddle cakes warm.

## Marinated Grilled Pork Loin with Orange Sauce

Serves 6
Working time: about 20 minutes
Total time: about 1 hour and 10 minutes
(includes marinating)

Calories **105**
Protein **12g**
Cholesterol **35mg**
Total fat **4g**
Saturated fat **1g**
Sodium **30mg**

| | | |
|---|---|---|
| 4 tbsp | frozen orange juice concentrate, thawed | 4 tbsp |
| 4 tbsp | malt vinegar | 4 tbsp |
| 2 | garlic cloves, finely chopped | 2 |
| | freshly ground black pepper | |
| 400 g | boneless pork loin, trimmed of fat and cut into 18 thin slices | 14 oz |

Mix together the orange juice concentrate, vinegar, garlic and some pepper in a large, shallow dish. Lay the slices of pork in the marinade, turning them over to coat them. Cover the dish and marinate the pork at room temperature for 1 hour or in the refrigerator for 3 hours.

If you plan to barbecue the pork, light the charcoal about 30 minutes before cooking time; to grill, pre-heat the grill for 10 minutes.

Remove the pork from the marinade. Transfer the marinade to a small saucepan and simmer it over medium-low heat until it has thickened slightly — about 3 minutes. Set the saucepan aside.

Grill or barbecue the pork slices until they are browned and no longer pink inside — about 1 minute on each side. Arrange the pork slices on a warmed serving platter. Briefly reheat the sauce and pour it over the meat. Serve at once.

## Salsa Verde

Makes about 35 cl (12 fl oz)
Working time: about 20 minutes
Total time: about 1 hour and 20 minutes
(includes chilling)

Per 4 tablespoons:
Calories **16**
Protein **0g**
Cholesterol **0mg**
Total fat **0g**
Saturated fat **0g**
Sodium **4mg**

| | | |
|---|---|---|
| 250 g | green tomatoes, seeded and finely chopped | 8 oz |
| 1 | fresh hot green chili pepper, seeded, deribbed and finely chopped (caution, opposite page) | 1 |
| 3 | garlic cloves, finely chopped | 3 |
| 1 | small onion, finely chopped | 1 |
| 4 tbsp | fresh lime juice | 4 tbsp |
| 1 tbsp | chopped fresh coriander | 1 tbsp |

In a small bowl stir together all of the Ingredients. Cover the bowl with plastic film and refrigerate the salsa verde until it is cold — about 1 hour. Serve the salsa with the griddle cakes and the grilled pork.

## Individual Moulded Tomato Salads

Serves 6
Working time: about 1 hour
Total time: about 3 hours (includes chilling)

Calories **45**
Protein **3g**
Cholesterol **0mg**
Total fat **0g**
Saturated fat **0g**
Sodium **110mg**

| | | |
|---|---|---|
| 400 g | canned whole tomatoes, with their juice | 14 oz |
| 1 tbsp | powdered gelatine | 1 tbsp |
| 75 g | shelled fresh or frozen peas | . 2½ oz |
| 2 | sweet red peppers, seeded, deribbed and finely chopped | 2 |
| 3 | spring onions, trimmed and finely chopped | 3 |
| ⅓ | cucumber, peeled, seeded and finely chopped | ⅓ |
| 1 | stick celery, trimmed and finely chopped | 1 |
| 2 tbsp | fresh lemon juice | 2 tbsp |
| 1 tsp | sugar | 1 tsp |
| ½ tsp | Tabasco sauce | ½ tsp |
| ¼ tsp | salt | ¼ tsp |
| 125 g | lettuce, shredded | 4 oz |

Purée the tomatoes and their juice in a blender or food processor. Strain the purée and discard the seeds. Pour 30 cl (½ pint) of the purée into a large bowl.

Pour 12.5 cl (4 fl oz) of the remaining purée into a small saucepan; reserve any remaining purée for another use. Sprinkle the gelatine over the purée in the saucepan; let the gelatine stand until it is spongy — about 5 minutes. Place the pan over low heat and bring the purée to a simmer, whisking to dissolve the gelatine. Remove the mixture from the heat and set it aside.

If you are using fresh peas, cook them in boiling water until they are tender — about 3 minutes; frozen peas need only be thawed. Add the peas, peppers, spring onions, cucumber, celery, lemon juice, sugar, Tabasco sauce and salt to the purée in the bowl.

Pour the gelatine mixture into the bowl with the vegetables and stir well. Divide the tomato salad between six 17.5 cl (6 fl oz) ramekins. Refrigerate the ramekins until the tomato salad has set — at least 2 hours.

To serve, line six plates with the lettuce. Dip the bottoms of the ramekins in hot water, then invert the ramekins on to the lettuce and lift them from the salads.

EDITOR'S NOTE: *The salads can be unmoulded 2 hours in advance and kept in the refrigerator, covered with plastic film until serving time. This recipe can also be used to fill a single 1.25 litre (2 pint) mould*

# Strawberry and Grapefruit Salad

Serves 4
Working time: about 30 minutes
Total time: about 1 hour and 30 minutes
(includes chilling)

Calories **95**
Protein **1g**
Cholesterol **0mg**
Total fat **0g**
Saturated fat **0g**
Sodium **1mg**

| | | |
|---|---|---|
| 4 | grapefruits | 4 |
| 350 g | strawberries, hulled, halved if large | 12 oz |
| 3 tbsp | Triple Sec or other orange-flavoured liqueur | 3 tbsp |
| 4 tbsp | caster sugar | 4 tbsp |
| | mint sprigs for garnish (optional) | |

Use a sharp knife to slice off both ends of one of the grapefruits so that the flesh just shows through. With the grapefruit standing on a flat end, cut round the flesh, following the contour of the fruit, to remove vertical strips of the peel and pith *(page 25)*. Working over a bowl to catch the juice, hold the peeled grapefruit in one hand and carefully slice between the flesh and membrane to free each segment; let the segments fall into the bowl. Remove the seeds from the segments and discard them. Squeeze any remaining juice from the membrane into the bowl. Repeat these steps with the remaining grapefruits.

Put the strawberries, liqueur and sugar into the bowl with the grapefruit segments and juice; toss the fruit gently with a wooden spoon. Cover the fruit and chill it thoroughly — at least 1 hour. Serve the salad in chilled bowls, garnished with mint sprigs if you like.

---

### Chili Peppers — a Cautionary Note

Both dried and fresh hot chili peppers should be handled with care. Their flesh and seeds contain volatile oils that can make skin tingle and cause eyes to burn. Rubber gloves offer protection — but the cook should still be careful not to touch the face, lips or eyes when working with chili peppers.

Soaking fresh chili peppers in cold, salted water for an hour will remove some of their fire. If canned chilies are substituted for fresh ones, they should be rinsed in cold water in order to eliminate as much of the brine used to preserve them as possible.

# Pink Lime Freeze

Makes 6 servings
Working time: about 15 minutes
Total time: about 2 hours and 15 minutes
(includes freezing)

Calories **75**
Protein **0g**
Cholesterol **0mg**
Total fat **0g**
Saturated fat **0g**
Sodium **2mg**

| | | |
|---|---|---|
| 100 g | sugar | 3½ oz |
| 17.5 cl | fresh lime juice | 6 fl oz |
| 1 | large ripe tomato, skinned, seeded and puréed, or 12.5 cl (4 fl oz) unsalted tomato juice | 1 |
| 6 | thin lime slices for garnish | 6 |

Pour ¼ litre (8 fl oz) of water into a saucepan and stir in the sugar. Bring the mixture to the boil, reduce the heat, and simmer for 2 minutes. Transfer the syrup to a shallow pan and stir in ¾ litre (1¼ pints) of cold water, the lime juice and tomato purée. Freeze the liquid for at least 2 hours, stirring it every half hour.

Just before serving, break the frozen mixture into chunks and process them in two batches in a blender until the mixture is smooth but slushy. Pour the drink into six chilled glasses and garnish each one with a slice of lime.

---

### WINTER BRUNCH

———

*Grouper Stuffed with Pickled Vegetables*
*Broccoli Salad with Hot Red Pepper Vinaigrette*
*Haricot Bean and Potato Salad with Onions and Sage*
*Fennel Toast*
*Fresh Fruit Winter Salad*
*Cardamom and Ginger Coffee*

---

A great deal of the work for this winter brunch menu can be done the day before the brunch. Soak the beans and prepare the saged onions for the haricot bean and potato salad. Make the pickled vegetables for the fish stuffing, the fennel-onion mixture for the toast, and the fruit salad. Cut the broccoli and make the hot red pepper vinaigrette for the broccoli salad. Cover everything and store it in the refrigerator.

On the day of the brunch, cook the beans, onions and potatoes for the bean salad. Stuff the fish with the pickled vegetables and then bake the assembly. Partially cook the broccoli and, when it is cool, toss it with the hot red pepper vinaigrette. Slice the bread, spread on the fennel-onion mixture, and bake the slices until they are toasted.

## Grouper Stuffed with Pickled Vegetables

———

Serves 8
Working time: about 40 minutes
Total time: about 1 hour and 45 minutes

Calories **185**
Protein **25g**
Cholesterol **50mg**
Total fat **4g**
Saturated fat **1g**
Sodium **215mg**

| | | |
|---|---|---|
| 6 | carrots | 6 |
| ½ | small green cabbage, cored and very thinly sliced | ½ |
| 1 | onion, very thinly sliced | 1 |
| 12.5 cl | cider vinegar | 4 fl oz |
| 1 tbsp | sugar | 1 tbsp |
| 15 g | unsalted butter | ½ oz |
| 1 tbsp | safflower oil | 1 tbsp |
| 1½ tbsp | fresh lemon juice | 1½ tbsp |
| ¼ tsp | salt | ¼ tsp |
| | freshly ground black pepper | |
| 2.5 kg | grouper, sea bass, bass or John Dory, filleted and skinned | 5 lb |

To make the pickled vegetables, grate 4 of the carrots and put them, with the cabbage and onion, into a large bowl. Combine the vinegar and sugar in a small

---

*Carrot slices decorate a baked grouper stuffed with pickled vegetables and served with fennel toast, broccoli with a red pepper vinaigrette, and a hearty bean and potato salad. And, for a light, refreshing close — a mug of spiced coffee and a salad of winter fruits.*

saucepan and bring the liquid to the boil. Immediately pour the boiling liquid over the vegetables and toss the mixture well. Squeeze the vegetables firmly, toss them again, and then set them aside to marinate for about 20 minutes. Toss the vegetables again and squeeze them firmly to extract the excess liquid and discard it.

Preheat the oven to 170°C (325°F or Mark 3). In a small saucepan, warm the butter, oil, lemon juice, salt and pepper over low heat until the butter has melted. Brush a shallow baking dish large enough to accommodate the fish with some of the lemon butter. Place one of the fillets, skinned side down, in the dish. Brush some of the lemon butter over the fillet and then cover it evenly with the vegetables. Place the second fillet on the work surface skinned side up; brush the fillet with half of the remaining lemon butter. Place the fillet, buttered side down, on top of the vegetables. Brush the remaining lemon butter over the top and sides of the assembly. Bake the fish for 45 minutes.

In the meantime, prepare the carrot garnish. Thinly slice the 2 remaining carrots diagonally. Bring ½ litre (16 fl oz) of water to the boil in a small saucepan. Add the carrots and cook them just until they are tender — 4 to 5 minutes. Drain the carrots, refresh them under cold running water and set them aside.

When the fish is ready, remove it from the oven and let it stand while you bake the fennel toast. Garnish the stuffed fish with the carrot slices, arranging them in two rows down the centre.

## Broccoli Salad with Hot Red Pepper Vinaigrette

———

Serves 8
Working (and total) time: about 30 minutes

Calories **35**
Protein **2g**
Cholesterol **0mg**
Total fat **2g**
Saturated fat **0g**
Sodium **50mg**

| | | |
|---|---|---|
| 1⅛ tsp | salt | 1⅛ tsp |
| 750 g | broccoli, the florets separated from the stems, the stems peeled and sliced diagonally into 3 mm (⅛ inch) thick ovals | 1½ lb |
| 1 tbsp | fresh lemon juice | 1 tbsp |
| 1 tbsp | red wine vinegar | 1 tbsp |
| ¼ tsp | caster sugar | ¼ tsp |
| 1 tsp | mustard seeds, crushed | 1 tsp |
| ¼ to ½ tsp | dried hot red pepper flakes | ¼ to ½ tsp |
| 1 | garlic clove, very finely chopped | 1 |
| 1 tbsp | virgin olive oil | 1 tbsp |

Pour 2 litres (3½ pints) of water into a large pan and add 1 teaspoon of the salt; bring the water to the boil. Cook the broccoli in the boiling water for 2 minutes. Drain the broccoli and refresh it under cold running water. Transfer the broccoli to a baking sheet lined with a tea towel, spreading out the broccoli in a single layer, and let it drain thoroughly.

To make the vinaigrette, whisk together the lemon juice, the vinegar, the remaining salt and the sugar ▶

in a small bowl; stir in the mustard seeds, pepper flakes and garlic. Leave the mixture to stand for 5 minutes to let the flavours meld. Whisk in the olive oil.

Transfer the broccoli to a serving dish, pour the vinaigrette over the broccoli, and toss it well. Serve the salad immediately.

---

EDITOR'S NOTE: *You may prepare the broccoli and the vinaigrette up to 2 hours in advance. Store them in the refrigerator separately, then toss the broccoli with the vinaigrette at serving time.*

# Haricot Bean and Potato Salad with Onions and Sage

---

Serves 8
Working time: about 40 minutes
Total time: about 2 hours and 30 minutes
(includes soaking)

Calories **235**
Protein **12g**
Cholesterol **6mg**
Total fat **5g**
Saturated fat **1g**
Sodium **180mg**

| | | |
|---|---|---|
| 250 g | dried haricot beans, picked over and rinsed | 8 oz |
| 250 g | button onions, peeled | 8 oz |
| 6 tbsp | red wine vinegar | 6 tbsp |
| 2 tbsp | chopped fresh sage, or 2 tsp ground sage | 2 tbsp |
| 500 g | red potatoes, scrubbed, cut into 2 cm (¾ inch) pieces and covered with water | 1 lb |
| 60 g | mild back bacon, diced | 2 oz |
| ¼ tsp | salt | ¼ tsp |
| | freshly ground black pepper | |
| 1½ tbsp | olive oil, preferably virgin | 1½ tbsp |

Put the beans into a large heavy saucepan and pour in enough water to cover them by about 7.5 cm (3 inches). Discard any beans that float to the surface. Cover the pan, leaving the lid ajar, and bring the liquid to the boil. Boil the beans for 2 minutes, then turn off the heat, and let the beans soak for at least 1 hour.

Drain the beans and return them to the pan. Pour in enough water to cover them by 7.5 cm (3 inches). Bring the liquid to the boil. Reduce the heat to maintain a simmer, then cover the pan and cook the beans, stirring occasionally, until they are just tender — 1 to 1¼ hours.

While the beans are cooking, put the onions into a heavy-bottomed saucepan with 12.5 cl (4 fl oz) of water, 1 tablespoon of the vinegar and half of the sage; bring the mixture to the boil. Reduce the heat and simmer the onions, partially covered, until they are tender and almost all of the liquid has evaporated — approximately 15 minutes.

When the beans have finished cooking, drain them. Drain the potatoes and add them to the beans along with the bacon, the remaining sage, the salt and some pepper. Gently stir in the onions and 6 tablespoons of water. Cover the pan and cook the mixture over low heat, stirring every now and then, until the potatoes are tender and almost all of the liquid is absorbed — approximately 20 minutes.

Transfer the mixture to a large serving bowl and dribble the remaining vinegar over the salad. Toss the mixture, then add the oil, and toss gently again to coat all of the ingredients with the oil. Serve the salad hot, at room temperature or chilled.

## Fennel Toast

Serves 8
Working time: about 30 minutes
Total time: about 40 minutes

Calories **90**
Protein **24g**
Cholesterol **0mg**
Total fat **3g**
Saturated fat **1g**
Sodium **175mg**

| | | |
|---|---|---|
| 1 tbsp | virgin olive oil | 1 tbsp |
| 3 | garlic cloves, thinly sliced | 3 |
| 1 tbsp | fennel seeds, lightly crushed | 1 tbsp |
| 500 g | onion, chopped | 1 lb |
| ¼ tsp | salt | ¼ tsp |
| | freshly ground black pepper | |
| 2 tbsp | cider vinegar | 2 tbsp |
| 1 | loaf French bread | 1 |

Heat the oil in a heavy frying pan over medium-high heat. Add the garlic and the fennel seeds and sauté them just until the garlic begins to brown — about 1 minute. Add the onion, the salt and some pepper, and continue cooking, stirring frequently, until the onions are lightly browned — 10 to 15 minutes. Stir in the vinegar and cook the mixture for 1 minute more. Transfer the onion mixture to a bowl and let it cool slightly.

Slice the French bread into twenty-four 5 mm (¼ inch) thick rounds; reserve any remaining bread for another use. Spread the rounds with a thin layer of the onion mixture, placing each on a rack as it is finished. Cover the rack with plastic film and then set the rack aside until you are ready to bake the prepared bread rounds.

When the fish has finished baking, increase the oven's temperature to 200°C (400°F or Mark 6). Uncover the bread rounds and bake them until their edges are lightly browned — about 7 minutes. Surround the baked fish with the rounds, or transfer them to a serving plate, and serve them at once.

EDITOR'S NOTE: *These toast rounds are baked on a rack in order to prevent their bottoms from becoming soggy.*

## Fresh Fruit Winter Salad

Serves 8
Working time: about 25 minutes
Total time: about 1 hour and 15 minutes

Calories **105**
Protein **1g**
Cholesterol **0mg**
Total fat **0g**
Saturated fat **0g**
Sodium **3mg**

| | | |
|---|---|---|
| ¼ litre | fresh orange juice | 8 fl oz |
| 12.5 cl | dry white wine | 4 fl oz |
| 1½ tsp | grated orange rind | 1½ tsp |
| 45 g | stoned dates, chopped | 1½ oz |
| 75 g | raisins | 2½ oz |
| 2 | crisp red apples, quartered, cored and cut into 2 cm (¾ inch) pieces | 2 |
| 1 | large pear, quartered, cored and cut into 2 cm (¾ inch) pieces | 1 |
| 165 g | white, red or black grapes, halved and seeded | 5½ oz |

Put the orange juice, wine and orange rind into a heavy saucepan. Bring the mixture to a simmer over medium heat and cook it until it is reduced by half — 15 to 20 minutes. Add the dates and the raisins; continue cooking the mixture, stirring occasionally, for 3 minutes. Remove the pan from the heat.

Place the apple and pear pieces in a large bowl. Pour the hot orange juice mixture over the fresh fruit and toss the mixture well. Add the grapes and toss the salad again. Refrigerate the salad for 30 minutes. Toss the salad again just before serving.

EDITOR'S NOTE: *This salad will keep in the refrigerator for up to 24 hours. It can be served chilled or at room temperature.*

## Cardamom and Ginger Coffee

Serves 8
Working (and total) time: about 15 minutes

Calories **80**
Protein **2g**
Cholesterol **15mg**
Total fat **5g**
Saturated fat **3g**
Sodium **20mg**

| | | |
|---|---|---|
| 60 g | French roast or other strong roasted coffee beans, ground | 2 oz |
| 2 tsp | ground cardamom | 2 tsp |
| 3 tbsp | finely chopped fresh ginger root | 3 tbsp |
| ¼ litre | milk | 8 fl oz |
| 1½ tsp | sugar | 1½ tsp |
| 4 tbsp | double cream, well chilled | 4 tbsp |
| 30 g | plain chocolate, grated | 1 oz |

Combine the coffee, 1½ teaspoons of the cardamom, and the ginger; brew this mixture in a coffeepot with 1.75 litres (3 pints) of cold, fresh water.

While the coffee is brewing, put the milk and sugar into a small saucepan and heat them over low heat, stirring constantly, just until the milk is hot and steaming — about 5 minutes. When the coffee is ready, pour it and the hot milk into a large, warmed bowl.

In a separate bowl, add the remaining cardamom to the cream and whisk the mixture until it forms soft peaks. Spoon the whipped cream on to the coffee, sprinkle the chocolate on top, and serve.

The tomato and orange soup for this spring brunch can be prepared a day ahead of time and chilled. The meringues can be made ahead, too, and stored in an airtight container for several days. Steep the juice for the drink with the rosemary overnight. Prepare all of the salad ingredients and refrigerate them. If you like, the asparagus for the egg noodles can also be prepared the day before the brunch, providing the pieces are tightly covered and chilled.

On the day of the brunch, you can make the seafood sausage up to 4 hours before poaching it, but be sure to keep it chilled. Prepare the orange garnish for the soup. The fruit for the meringue can be sliced as much as 8 hours in advance; fill the meringues just before serving them. Poach the seafood sausage and cook the noodles. Toss the salad just before serving it.

# Cold Tomato and Orange Soup

Serves 6
Working time: about 30 minutes
Total time: about 1 hour and 30 minutes
(includes chilling)

Calories **120**
Protein **4g**
Cholesterol **2mg**
Total fat **3g**
Saturated fat **1g**
Sodium **85mg**

| | | |
|---|---|---|
| 1.25 kg | ripe tomatoes, skinned, seeded and cut into large pieces, or 800 g (28 oz) canned whole tomatoes, seeded, the juice reserved | 2½ lb |
| 2 | spring onions, trimmed, white parts chopped and green parts thinly sliced | 2 |
| 1 tbsp | fresh lemon juice | 1 tbsp |
| 2 tsp | virgin olive oil | 2 tsp |
| 2 tsp | honey | 2 tsp |
| ½ tsp | curry powder | ½ tsp |
| 1 tsp | finely chopped fresh ginger root | 1 tsp |
| ⅛ tsp | salt | ⅛ tsp |
| | freshly ground black pepper | |
| 30 cl | fresh orange juice | ½ pint |
| ¼ litre | plain low-fat yogurt | 8 fl oz |
| 1 | orange, peeled and segmented, for garnish | 1 |

Put the tomatoes and the white parts of the spring onions into a food processor or a blender. Add the lemon juice, olive oil, honey, curry powder, ginger, salt and a generous grinding of pepper. Process the mix-

ture until it is smooth. Transfer the mixture to a large bowl and whisk in the orange juice, the reserved tomato juice if you are using canned tomatoes, and the yogurt. Cover the soup and refrigerate it for at least 1 hour. To serve, ladle the soup into chilled bowls or cups and garnish each portion with the green spring onions. Carefully float one or two of the orange sections in each portion.

EDITOR'S NOTE: *This soup may be prepared as much as 24 hours in advance.*

# Scallop and Salmon Sausages with Asparagus and Noodles

Serves 6
Working (and total) time: about 1 hour and 45 minutes

Calories **360**
Protein **23g**
Cholesterol **95mg**
Total fat **10g**
Saturated fat **3g**
Sodium **330mg**

| | | |
|---|---|---|
| 2 | small carrots, cut into 1 cm (½ inch) pieces | 2 |
| 3 | slices of white bread | 3 |
| 6 tbsp | semi-skimmed milk | 6 tbsp |
| 1 | egg | 1 |
| 1¼ tsp | salt | 1¼ tsp |
| ⅛ tsp | grated nutmeg | ⅛ tsp |
| ⅛ tsp | cayenne pepper | ⅛ tsp |
| 1 | salmon steak (about 300 g/10 oz), skinned and boned, the bones reserved | 1 |
| 250 g | scallops, rinsed and patted dry, the bright white connective tissue removed and reserved | 8 oz |
| 2 tbsp | fresh lemon juice | 2 tbsp |
| 125 g | onion, chopped | 4 oz |
| 12.5 cl | dry white wine | 4 fl oz |
| 500 g | asparagus, trimmed and sliced diagonally into 5 cm (2 inch) pieces | 1 lb |
| 250 g | medium egg noodles | 8 oz |
| 10 g | unsalted butter | ⅓ oz |
| | freshly ground black pepper | |

In a small saucepan, bring ½ litre (16 fl oz) of water to the boil. Add the carrot pieces and cook them until they are soft — about 10 minutes. Drain the carrots, then refresh them under cold water. Drain the carrots again and set them aside.

Tear each slice of bread into four or five pieces and put the pieces into a food processor. Process the bread until it turns into fine crumbs — about 30 seconds. Pour in the milk, then add the egg, ⅛ teaspoon of the salt, the nutmeg and the cayenne pepper. Process the mixture for about 5 seconds to combine the ingredients thoroughly.

Add the carrots and process the mixture, using ▶

*Cold tomato and orange soup is followed by scallop and salmon sausages on a bed of spring asparagus and egg noodles, a salad of watercress and peppers, and fruit-filled meringue with a lattice top. Tangerine mimosas are served from a bowl garnished with rosemary and tangerine slices.*

several short bursts of power, until the carrots are chopped into very small pieces. Transfer the mixture to a bowl, cover the bowl, and put it into the refrigerator to chill. At the same time, put a large, empty bowl into the refrigerator to chill.

Cut the salmon steak into 2.5 cm (1 inch) chunks and put them, along with the scallops, into the food processor. Process the salmon and scallops until they are finely chopped — about 20 seconds. Transfer the salmon-scallop mixture to the chilled bowl and stir in 1½ tablespoons of the lemon juice. With a wooden spoon, work in the breadcrumb mixture, half at a time, until the two mixtures are well blended. Cover the bowl and refrigerate it.

To start preparing the sauce, put the reserved salmon bones and the connective tissue of the scallops into a heavy-bottomed saucepan with the onion, white wine, ⅛ teaspoon of the salt and ¼ litre (8 fl oz) of water. Bring to the boil, then lower the heat, and simmer the mixture until it is reduced by half — about 20 minutes. Strain the liquid through a sieve into a bowl, gently pushing down on the solids to extract all the liquid; discard the contents of the sieve. Return the strained liquid to the saucepan and set it aside.

While the liquid is reducing, make the sausages. Divide the salmon-scallop mixture in half. Arrange one half in a line near one of the long edges of a piece of strong aluminium foil about 45 cm (18 inches) long, and form a sausage about 30 cm (12 inches) long, following the technique shown on page 77. Repeat the procedure with the remaining half of the salmon-scallop mixture to form a second sausage.

Pour enough water into a heavy fireproof casserole to fill it 2.5 cm (1 inch) deep. Bring the water to the boil, then reduce the heat to maintain a low simmer. Put the sausages into the casserole and poach them for 20 minutes, carefully turning them over after 10 minutes. Using two slotted spoons, remove the sausages from the water and set them aside; do not remove the aluminium foil.

While the sausages are poaching, prepare the asparagus and noodles. Bring 2 litres (3½ pints) of water to the boil with the remaining salt; add the asparagus pieces and blanch them for 1 minute. Remove the asparagus with a slotted spoon and set it aside. Add the noodles to the boiling water. Start testing them after 5 minutes and continue to cook them until they are *al dente*. Drain the noodles and transfer them to a large heated serving platter. Scatter the asparagus over the noodles.

Remove the sausages from the foil and slice them into 1 cm (½ inch) thick rounds. Arrange the sausage rounds in several rows on top of the noodles and asparagus. Keep the platter warm while you finish preparing the sauce.

Place the pan containing the sauce over medium heat. Whisk in the butter, along with the remaining lemon juice and a generous grinding of pepper. When the butter is blended in, pour the hot sauce over the noodles and sausages. Serve the dish immediately.

# Watercress and Red Pepper Salad

Serves 6
Working time: about 15 minutes
Total time: about 20 minutes

Calories **50**
Protein **0g**
Cholesterol **0mg**
Total fat **5g**
Saturated fat **1g**
Sodium **50mg**

| | | |
|---|---|---|
| 1½ tbsp | fresh lemon juice | 1½ tbsp |
| 1 tbsp | fresh orange juice | 1 tbsp |
| 1 tbsp | red wine vinegar | 1 tbsp |
| ½ tsp | grated lemon rind | ½ tsp |
| ⅛ tsp | salt | ⅛ tsp |
| | freshly ground black pepper | |
| 2 | shallots, thinly sliced | 2 |
| 2 tbsp | virgin olive oil | 2 tbsp |
| 2 | sweet red peppers, seeded, deribbed and thinly sliced into 5 cm (2 inch) long strips | 2 |
| 1 | bunch watercress, trimmed, washed and dried | 1 |

Whisk together the lemon juice, orange juice, vinegar, lemon rind, salt and some pepper in a large bowl. Add the shallots and let the mixture stand for 5 minutes so that the flavours can meld. Stir in the olive oil.

Add the pepper strips to the bowl containing the shallot vinaigrette and toss the mixture well. Add the watercress and toss again. Serve the salad at once.

## Strawberry and Kiwi Fruit Meringue

Serves 6
Working time: about 35 minutes
Total time: about 4 hours and 30 minutes
(includes slow baking)

Calories **145**
Protein **2g**
Cholesterol **0mg**
Total fat **0g**
Saturated fat **0g**
Sodium **30mg**

| | | |
|---|---|---|
| 3 | egg whites | 3 |
| 150 g | plus 1 tbsp sugar | 5 oz |
| 175 to 350 g | strawberries, hulled | 6 to 12 oz |
| 3 | kiwi fruits, peeled and sliced into six slices each | 3 |

Line a baking sheet with parchment paper or with a brown paper bag that has been cut open and flattened. Preheat the oven to 70°C (160°F). (If your oven does not have a setting this low, set it just below 100°C/200°F.) Keep the oven door propped open with a ball of crumpled foil.

To prepare the meringue, put the egg whites and 150 g (5 oz) of the sugar into a large metal bowl. Set the bowl over, but not in, a pan of steaming water, and whisk the mixture often to dissolve the sugar completely — 5 to 6 minutes. Remove the bowl from the heat.

Using an electric mixer, beat the egg whites on medium-high speed until they form stiff peaks and have cooled to room temperature. Transfer the meringue to a piping bag fitted with a 1 cm (½ inch) star nozzle.

Holding the nozzle about 1 cm (½ inch) above the baking sheet, pipe a tightly coiled spiral of meringue until you have formed a disc about 18 cm (7 inches) across. Pipe a single ring of meringue on top of the disc's edge, forming a low wall that will hold in the fruit filling. On the same baking sheet, pipe an open circle 15 cm (6 inches) in diameter. Pipe three evenly spaced meringue strips across the circle. Pipe three more strips diagonal to the first three to create a lattice pattern.

Bake the meringues until they have thoroughly dried out but are still white — at least 4 hours. Remove the meringues from the oven and let them cool to room temperature on the baking sheet — they will be quite crisp. The meringues can be made ahead and stored in an airtight container, with a piece of greaseproof paper separating them, for up to two days; in humid weather, however, it is best to use them right away.

Before assembling the meringue, purée 125 g (4 oz) of the strawberries with the remaining 1 tablespoon of sugar in a food processor or a blender. Set the berry purée aside. Thinly slice the remaining strawberries and reserve them.

Just before serving, pour the berry purée into the meringue shell. Make a border of the sliced kiwi fruits around the inside of the meringue shell and then arrange the sliced strawberries in a spiral pattern inside the border. Place the lattice top over the fruit-filled meringue at a slight angle. Serve at once.

## Tangerine Mimosas

Serves 6
Working time: about 10 minutes
Total time: about 8 hours and 10 minutes (includes chilling)

Calories **140**
Protein **1g**
Cholesterol **0mg**
Total fat **0g**
Saturated fat **0g**
Sodium **5mg**

| | | |
|---|---|---|
| ¾ litre | fresh tangerine or orange juice | 1¼ pints |
| 12.5 cl | white grape juice | 4 fl oz |
| 2 | sprigs fresh rosemary, or 1 tbsp dried rosemary | 2 |
| ½ litre | chilled dry champagne | 16 fl oz |
| 1 | tangerine or orange, thinly sliced | 1 |

In a bowl, mix the tangerine or orange juice, the grape juice and the rosemary; cover the bowl and refrigerate it for 8 hours or overnight to let the flavours meld. To serve, pour the juice into a punch bowl. (If using dried rosemary, strain the juice into the bowl.) To preserve as much of the champagne's effervescence as possible, pour it slowly down the side of the bowl; float the fruit slices in the punch and serve it in champagne flutes.

EDITOR'S NOTE: *If you like, place the punch bowl in a larger bowl filled with ice when you are ready to serve the mimosas.*

*Artichoke wedges form a dramatic garnish for a fresh
tuna summer salad, served with red pepper dressing and
peppered bread sticks. Frozen cucumber boats filled with
cucumber sorbet, a cherry summer pudding and a pitcher
of apple juice complete the brunch.*

---

**SUMMER BRUNCH**

———

*Minted Cucumber Sorbet*
*Summer Salad with Fresh Tuna*
*Peppered Bread Sticks*
*Cherry Summer Pudding*

---

Most of the work for this summer brunch can be done ahead of time. The bread sticks can be made up to two weeks in advance and then frozen; alternatively, bake them the day before the brunch and, when they have cooled, store them in a sealed paper bag. Prepare the sorbet and the cherry pudding a day beforehand; freeze the sorbet and chill the pudding. The red pepper dressing, artichokes, beans, potatoes, tuna and greens for the tuna salad also can be prepared a day ahead and kept separately, covered, in the refrigerator.

On the day of the brunch, unmould the cherry pudding. Dress the greens for the tuna salad and then arrange all of its prepared components. If the sorbet is frozen solid, put it in the refrigerator to soften for 30 minutes before serving it.

# Minted Cucumber Sorbet

THIS PALATE-AWAKENING SORBET GETS
THE BRUNCH UNDER WAY.

---

Serves 6
Working time: about 30 minutes
Total time: 1 to 3 hours, depending
on freezing method

Calories **75**
Protein **0g**
Cholesterol **0mg**
Total fat **0g**
Saturated fat **0g**
Sodium **90mg**

| | | |
|---|---|---|
| 3 | large cucumbers | 3 |
| 100 g | sugar | 3½ oz |
| ¼ tsp | salt | ¼ tsp |
| 4 tbsp | cider vinegar | 4 tbsp |
| 1 tbsp | chopped fresh mint, or 1½ tsp dried mint | 1 tbsp |
| 6 | mint sprigs for garnish (optional) | 6 |

Peel, seed and slice two of the cucumbers. Scrub the remaining cucumber and chill it in the refrigerator.

In a small saucepan, bring 12.5 cl (4 fl oz) of water and the sugar to the boil over medium-high heat and cook the syrup for 2 minutes. Add the sliced cucumbers, salt and vinegar to the saucepan, reduce the heat to medium and simmer the mixture, stirring frequently, for 5 minutes. The cucumbers should be translucent. Remove the pan from the heat and stir in ▶

the chopped or dried mint. Purée the cucumber mixture in a blender or food processor and set it aside to cool.

Freeze the purée in an ice cream maker according to the manufacturer's instructions. (Alternatively, the sorbet can be still-frozen in a shallow dish covered with plastic film. Stir the sorbet with a whisk every 30 minutes to break up the large ice crystals.)

Meanwhile, prepare the cucumber boats. Using a vegetable peeler or a cannelle knife, peel stripes down the length of the remaining cucumber *(page 125)*. Cut the cucumber in half lengthwise. With a melon baller or small spoon, scoop out the centres of the cucumber pieces leaving the bottoms intact and 5 mm (¼ inch) of flesh on the sides, then cut each half crosswise into three equal pieces. Thoroughly chill the boats.

Spoon the frozen sorbet into the cucumber boats, mounding it, and return them to the freezer until serving time. If the boats remain in the freezer for more than 1 hour, allow them to stand at room temperature for about 15 minutes to soften the sorbet slightly. If you wish, garnish each boat with a sprig of mint.

# Summer Salad with Fresh Tuna

THIS UPDATE OF THE CLASSIC *SALADE NIÇOISE* REPLACES THE STANDARD OILY VINAIGRETTE WITH A SPRIGHTLY DRESSING BASED ON ROASTED RED PEPPERS.

Serves 6
Working (and total) time: about 2 hours

Calories **250**
Protein **14g**
Cholesterol **15mg**
Total fat **11g**
Saturated fat **2g**
Sodium **270mg**

| | | |
|---|---|---|
| 2 | globe artichokes | 2 |
| 1 | lemon, halved | 1 |
| 125 g | fresh French beans, trimmed and cut into 4 cm (1 ½ inch) pieces | 4 oz |
| 75 g | shelled fresh or frozen peas | 2½ oz |
| 6 | red potatoes (about 500 g/1 lb), scrubbed | 6 |
| 250 g | fresh tuna steak (or swordfish), about 1 cm (½ inch) thick | 8 oz |
| 250 g | assorted salad greens (such as oak leaf, endive and cos lettuce, spinach, watercress, chicory or radicchio), washed, dried and torn into pieces if necessary | 8 oz |
| 12 | cherry tomatoes, halved | 12 |
| 1 | small red onion, thinly sliced | 1 |
| **Red pepper dressing** | | |
| 2 | large sweet red peppers | 2 |
| 3 tbsp | virgin olive oil | 3 tbsp |
| 8 | oil-cured black olives, stoned | 8 |
| 3 | garlic cloves, chopped | 3 |
| 6 tbsp | fresh lemon juice | 6 tbsp |
| 15 g | parsley leaves | ½ oz |
| ¼ tsp | salt | ¼ tsp |
| | freshly ground black pepper | |

Preheat the grill. Place the peppers for the dressing about 5 cm (2 inches) below the preheated grill. Turn them as their sides become slightly scorched. When the peppers are blistered all over, put them into a bowl, cover them with plastic film and set them aside to cool; the trapped steam will loosen the skins.

While the peppers are cooling, trim the artichokes. Cut 2.5 cm (1 inch) off the tops, snip off the prickly leaf tips with kitchen scissors, then cut off the stems *(page 125)*. Rub the cut edges with a lemon half. Pour enough water into a large, non-reactive saucepan to fill it about 2.5 cm (1 inch) deep; add the lemon halves and stand the artichokes upright in the water. Cover the pan and bring the water to the boil, then reduce the heat to medium low. Steam the artichokes until a knife slides easily into the stem end and a leaf gently tugged pulls free easily — about 30 minutes. Refresh the artichokes under cold running water and set them upside down on paper towels to drain.

Meanwhile, pour enough water into another large saucepan to fill it 2.5 cm (1 inch) deep. Set a vegetable steamer in the pan, and put the French beans into the steamer along with the fresh peas, if you are using them. Cover the pan and bring the water to the boil over medium-high heat. Steam the vegetables until they are just tender — about 4 minutes. Lift the steamer from the saucepan but leave the water in the pan to use again. Refresh the French beans and the fresh peas under cold running water, then put them into a bowl. If you are using frozen peas, add them at this point. Cover the vegetables with plastic film and refrigerate them.

Add water to the saucepan, if necessary, to bring the level back to 2.5 cm (1 inch). Replace the steamer, add the potatoes, and steam them until they are tender — about 15 minutes.

To make the dressing, use a paring knife to peel the peppers and slice them open. Remove the stems, ribs and seeds, working over a bowl to catch any juices. Put the peppers into a blender or a food processor along with the pepper juices, oil, olives, garlic, lemon juice, parsley, salt and a generous grinding of black pepper. Purée the mixture.

Remove the cooked potatoes from the steamer and let them cool slightly. Cut the potatoes into 1 cm (½ inch) cubes, put them into a bowl, and toss them with 15 cl (¼ pint) of the dressing. Set the bowl aside.

Preheat the grill again. Rinse the tuna under cold running water and pat it dry with paper towels. Grill the tuna until its flesh is opaque and feels firm to the touch — about 3 minutes per side. Cut the fish into 1 cm (½ inch) chunks and toss them gently with the dressed potatoes. Cover the bowl with plastic film and refrigerate the mixture.

Cut the artichokes in half lengthwise and remove the hairy chokes with a small spoon or paring knife. Cut each half into three pieces.

In a large bowl, toss the greens with all but approximately 12.5 cl (4 fl oz) of the remaining dressing; line a large chilled serving platter with them. Arrange the potato-tuna salad, artichokes and tomatoes on the greens, then scatter the beans, peas and onion slices over the top. Pass the remaining dressing as a dip for the artichoke leaves.

# Peppered Bread Sticks

Makes 12 bread sticks
Working time: about 20 minutes
Total time: about 1 hour

Per bread stick:
Calories **110**
Protein **3g**
Cholesterol **0mg**
Total fat **1g**
Saturated fat **0g**
Sodium **180mg**

| | | |
|---|---|---|
| 1 tbsp | easy-blend dried yeast | 1 tbsp |
| ½ tsp | salt | ½ tsp |
| 150 g | plain flour | 5 oz |
| 4 tbsp | strong plain flour | 4 tbsp |
| ½ tsp | freshly ground black pepper | ½ tsp |
| 1 tsp | olive oil | 1 tsp |
| 3 tbsp | cornmeal | 3 tbsp |

Combine the yeast, salt, 25 g (4 oz) of the plain flour, the strong flour and the pepper in a large bowl. Heat 12.5 cl (4 oz) of water and the oil in a saucepan just until they are hot to the touch (43°C/110°F). Stir the hot water and oil into the flour mixture to combine the ingredients thoroughly.

Turn the dough out on to a floured surface and knead in the remaining plain flour. Continue to knead the dough until it is smooth and elastic — 4 to 5 minutes more.

Gather the dough into a ball and place it in a lightly oiled large bowl, turning the ball once to coat it with the oil. Cover the bowl with a damp towel or plastic film and let the dough rise in a warm, draught-free place until it has doubled in bulk — 30 to 40 minutes.

When the dough has risen, punch it down, then transfer it to a floured surface, and knead it for 2 minutes. Divide the dough into 12 equal pieces. Roll each piece into a 25 cm (10 inch) long rope.

Preheat the oven to 200°C (400°F or Mark 6). Sprinkle a baking sheet with the cornmeal. Lay the dough ropes on the sheet, cover them with the towel or plastic film and let the ropes rise in a warm place for 10 minutes.

Bake the bread sticks until they are dry and lightly browned — 10 to 15 minutes. Transfer them to a rack to cool or serve them at once, piping hot. If you plan to use the bread sticks the following day, store them in an airtight container.

# Cherry Summer Pudding

Serves 6
Working time: about 1 hour
Total time: about 9 hours (includes chilling)

Calories **290**
Protein **6g**
Cholesterol **0mg**
Total fat **3g**
Saturated fat **1g**
Sodium **255mg**

| | | |
|---|---|---|
| 600 g | stoned fresh or frozen sweet cherries | 1¼ lb |
| 6 tbsp | honey | 6 tbsp |
| 2 tbsp | fresh lemon juice | 2 tbsp |
| 26 | very thin slices white bread, crusts removed | 26 |
| 150 g | fresh cherries for garnish (optional) | 5 oz |

Put the 600 g (1¼ lb) of fresh or frozen cherries into a non-reactive saucepan. Add the honey and lemon juice to the saucepan; bring the mixture to the boil. Reduce the heat and simmer the cherries for 10 minutes. Purée the cherries in a blender or a food processor.

Spoon enough of the purée into a 1.5 litre (2½ pint) mould or bowl to coat the bottom. Cover the purée with a single layer of bread, trimming the slices to allow them to fit snugly. Fill the mould with alternating layers of cherry purée and bread, pouring any remaining purée over the last layer. Cover the mould with plastic film and put it into the refrigerator for at least 8 hours or overnight.

To serve the pudding, run a knife round the edge of the mould and set an inverted plate over it. Turn both over together and lift off the mould, gently shaking it until the pudding slides out. Garnish the pudding with the fresh cherries if you are using them.

slices. Add the apple slices to the salad along with the oil, salt and some pepper. Toss the salad and serve it immediately.

<table>
<tr><td colspan="2" align="center">**AUTUMN BRUNCH**</td></tr>
<tr><td colspan="2" align="center">———</td></tr>
<tr><td colspan="2" align="center">*Apple-Cabbage Salad*<br>*Sweetcorn Crêpes Filled with Turkey Fricassee*<br>*Mashed Sweet Potatoes with Sherry and Chestnuts*<br>*Pear and Cranberry Flan*</td></tr>
</table>

Except for some final steps, all of the work for this autumn brunch can be done a day ahead of time. Make the crêpes, the parsley-pepper sauce and the turkey fricassee. Assemble the salad, but do not add the oil, apples, salt and pepper. Combine the mashed sweet potatoes with the sherry and chestnuts so that the dish is ready to bake on the following day. Bake the tart shell and prepare the cranberry filling. Cover everything and store it in the refrigerator overnight.

All that remains to do on the day of the brunch is to bring the crêpes to room temperature and then fill them with hot turkey fricassee, bake the sweet potatoes, warm the parsley-pepper sauce, and add the apples, oil, salt and pepper to the salad. To finish the dessert, pour the cranberry filling into the tart shell, arrange the pear slices on top, and bake the tart.

# Apple-Cabbage Salad

Serves 6
Working time: about 20 minutes
Total time: about 25 minutes

Calories **70**
Protein **1g**
Cholesterol **0mg**
Total fat **2g**
Saturated fat **0g**
Sodium **105mg**

| | | |
|---|---|---|
| 600 g | green cabbage, shredded or thinly sliced | 1¼ lb |
| 4 tbsp | distilled white vinegar | 4 tbsp |
| 1 tbsp | sugar | 1 tbsp |
| 1 tbsp | pickling spice | 1 tbsp |
| 2 | red apples | 2 |
| 2 tsp | safflower oil | 2 tsp |
| ¼ tsp | salt | ¼ tsp |
| | freshly ground black pepper | |

Put the cabbage into a large serving bowl. To make the dressing, put the vinegar, sugar and pickling spice into a small saucepan and bring the liquid to a simmer over medium-high heat; stir the mixture several times to help dissolve the sugar. Simmer the dressing for 2 minutes. Hold a strainer over the cabbage, then pour the dressing through the strainer. Toss the salad well, then refrigerate it.

When you are ready to serve the salad, quarter and core the apples. Cut each quarter crosswise into thin

---

*Nestled sweetcorn crêpes filled with turkey fricassee and topped with parsley-pepper sauce make an attractive main course for this autumn brunch. Mashed sweet potatoes with sherry and chestnuts and an apple-cabbage salad provide seasonal accompaniments. Dessert is a pear and cranberry flan.*

# Sweetcorn Crêpes Filled with Turkey Fricassee

Serves 6
Working time: about 35 minutes
Total time: about 1 hour and 15 minutes

Calories **375**
Protein **33g**
Cholesterol **110mg**
Total fat **11g**
Saturated fat **3g**
Sodium **265mg**

| | | |
|---|---|---|
| 250 g | fresh sweetcorn kernels (about two small ears), or frozen sweetcorn kernels, thawed | 8 oz |
| 30 cl | skimmed milk | ½ pint |
| 1 | egg yolk | 1 |
| ⅛ tsp | salt | ⅛ tsp |
| ⅛ tsp | white pepper | ⅛ tsp |
| 15 g | unsalted butter, melted | ½ oz |
| 125 g | plain flour | 4 oz |
| ¼ tsp | safflower oil | ¼ tsp |
| | **Turkey fricassee** | |
| 750 g | turkey breast meat, diced | 1½ lb |
| ⅛ tsp | salt | ⅛ tsp |
| | freshly ground black pepper | |
| 1½ tbsp | safflower oil | 1½ tbsp |
| 1 | sweet green pepper, seeded, deribbed and finely chopped | 1 |
| 2 | onions, finely chopped | 2 |
| 250 g | mushrooms, wiped clean and finely chopped | 8 oz |
| 12.5 cl | dry vermouth or dry white wine | 4 fl oz |
| 4 tbsp | plain flour | 4 tbsp |
| 35 cl | unsalted chicken stock (recipe, page 138) | 12 fl oz |
| 1 tsp | fresh thyme, or ½ tsp dried thyme | 1 tsp |
| | **Parsley-pepper sauce** | |
| 35 cl | unsalted chicken stock (recipe, page 138) | 12 fl oz |
| 1½ tbsp | cornflour, mixed with 1 tbsp water | 1½ tbsp |
| ¼ tsp | freshly ground black pepper | ¼ tsp |
| ⅛ tsp | salt | ⅛ tsp |
| 2 tbsp | chopped parsley | 2 tbsp |

To make the crêpe batter, put the sweetcorn, milk, egg yolk, salt, pepper and butter into a food processor or a blender and purée them. There should be 45 cl (¾ pint) of the mixture; if there is less, add enough milk to make 45 cl (¾ pint) of liquid. Transfer the mixture to a bowl and gradually add the flour, whisking until the batter is smooth. Cover the bowl and let it stand for 1 hour. Alternatively, refrigerate the batter, covered, overnight; if the batter has thickened at the end of the refrigeration period, stir in additional milk, 1 tablespoon at a time, until the batter has thinned to its original consistency.

To prepare the turkey fricassee, toss the turkey, the salt and a generous grinding of pepper together in a bowl. Set the bowl aside.

Heat the oil in a large, heavy frying pan over medium heat. Add the green pepper, onions and mushrooms ▶

and cook the mixture, stirring occasionally, until the onion is translucent and the green pepper is soft — about 7 minutes. Add the vermouth or wine, and cook the mixture until almost all of the liquid has evaporated — 3 to 4 minutes. Sprinkle the flour over the vegetables, then pour in the stock. Stir the mixture until it is well blended. Add the turkey and the thyme, then reduce the heat, and simmer the mixture, partially covered, until the turkey firms up and turns white, indicating that it is cooked through — about 4 minutes. Remove the pan from the heat; keep it warm while you prepare the sauce.

To make the parsley-pepper sauce, bring the stock to a simmer in a small saucepan. Stir in the cornflour mixture, pepper and salt, and simmer the liquid for 6 minutes. Stir in the parsley, then cover the sauce, and keep it warm while you prepare the crêpes.

Heat a 15 cm (6 inch) crêpe pan or non-stick frying pan over medium-high heat. Add the ¼ teaspoon of oil and spread it over the entire surface with a paper towel. Pour about 2 tablespoons of the crêpe batter into the hot pan and immediately swirl the pan to coat the bottom with a thin, even layer of batter. Pour any excess batter back into the bowl. Cook the crêpe until the bottom is set — about 1 minute. Lift the edge with a spatula and turn the crêpe over, then cook the crêpe on the second side until it too is set — 15 to 30 seconds. Slide the crêpe on to a warmed plate; cover the crêpe and keep it warm. Repeat the process with the remaining batter, brushing the pan lightly with more oil if the crêpes begin to stick. Transfer the cooked crêpes to the plate as you go, separating them with pieces of greaseproof paper. There should be 12 crêpes in all.

Place about 4 tablespoons of the filling in a line down the centre of a crêpe and roll the crêpe to enclose the filling. Transfer the filled crêpe to a warmed serving platter. Repeat the process with the remaining crêpes and filling. Spoon the warm parsley-pepper sauce over the crêpes and serve them at once.

# Mashed Sweet Potatoes with Sherry and Chestnuts

Serves 6
Working time: about 20 minutes
Total time: about 1 hour

Calories **265**
Protein **5g**
Cholesterol **1mg**
Total fat **3g**
Saturated fat **0g**
Sodium **135mg**

| | | |
|---|---|---|
| 250 g | fresh chestnuts | 8 oz |
| 1 kg | orange-fleshed sweet potatoes, peeled and cut into 2.5 cm (1 inch) slices | 2 lb |
| 35 cl | skimmed milk | 12 fl oz |
| ¼ tsp | salt | ¼ tsp |
| ⅛ tsp | white pepper | ⅛ tsp |
| 2 tsp | safflower oil | 2 tsp |
| 1 tsp | finely chopped shallots | 1 tsp |
| 17.5 cl | dry sherry | 6 fl oz |

Lay a chestnut with its flat side down on a cutting board. Using a sharp paring knife, make an X in the rounded side of the shell, cutting through both the shell and the inner skin. Repeat the process with the other chestnuts. Cook the chestnuts in boiling water for 10 minutes. Remove the pan from the heat but do not drain the chestnuts. Alternatively, bake them in a 180°C (350°F or Mark 4) oven on a baking sheet until the cut shells begin to curl — about 15 minutes.

While the chestnuts are still warm, remove the shells and as much of the brown skin as possible. (Waiting until the chestnuts are cool would make them difficult to peel.) Finely chop the chestnuts and set them aside.

Preheat the oven to 180°C (350°F or Mark 4).

Pour enough water into a saucepan to fill it 2.5 cm (1 inch) deep. Set a steamer in the pan and put the sweet potatoes into the steamer. Bring the water to the boil, and steam the sweet potatoes, covered, until they are tender — about 10 minutes. Transfer them to a bowl.

Pour the milk into a saucepan and bring it just to a simmer. Add the milk to the sweet potatoes. Mash the sweet potatoes until they form a smooth purée, then stir in the salt and white pepper.

Heat the oil in a small, heavy frying pan set over medium-high heat. Add the shallots and cook them until they are translucent — about 1 minute. Stir in the chopped chestnuts and the sherry; simmer the mixture until the sherry has reduced by half — about 3 minutes. Combine this mixture with the sweet potatoes, then transfer them to a baking dish. Smooth the surface of the purée with a spatula. Bake the sweet potatoes until they are heated through — about 15 minutes. Serve at once.

Meanwhile, put the cranberries into a small saucepan with just enough water to float the berries; bring the liquid to a simmer and cook the cranberries until they burst — about 4 minutes. Drain the cranberries to remove any excess liquid and put them in a blender or food processor; add the orange juice and 3 tablespoons of the granulated sugar. Process the cranberries just until they are puréed. (Take care not to overprocess the cranberries. Crushing the seeds can make the purée bitter.) Strain the purée through a fine sieve to remove the seeds and skins; chill the purée.

To form the flan shell, set the chilled dough on a floured surface. Using a rolling pin, flatten the ball of dough into a round, then roll the dough into a 25 cm (10 inch) circle. Transfer the dough to a 20 cm (8 inch) flan tin with a removable bottom, rolling the dough around the rolling pin and then unrolling it on to the flan tin. Gently press the dough into the corners and up the sides of the flan tin. Fold any excess dough back into the tin and press it well into the sides. Chill the flan shell for 10 minutes.

Preheat the oven to 220°C (425°F or Mark 7).

To prebake the flan shell, put the flan tin on a baking sheet. Prick the bottom of the dough several times with a fork. Line the flan shell with a round of greaseproof paper and fill it with dried beans; this helps the pastry keep its shape. Bake the pastry for 10 minutes, remove the beans and greaseproof paper, and continue baking until the flan shell is dry and just begins to colour — about 5 minutes more. Remove the shell from the oven and let it cool in the flan tin.

Meanwhile, make a sugar syrup: heat the remaining granulated sugar with 2 tablespoons of water in a small saucepan over medium-low heat until the sugar is dissolved — 3 to 4 minutes.

To assemble the flan, fill the bottom of the cooled flan shell with the cranberry purée. Arrange the pear slices on top in a circular pattern, overlapping the pieces slightly. Brush the pears and the edge of the pastry with the sugar syrup. Sprinkle the top with the hazelnuts if you are using them. Bake the flan until the pears are soft and glazed — about 10 minutes. Remove the flan from the tin and serve it hot or cold.

# Pear and Cranberry Flan

Serves 6
Working time: about 25 minutes
Total time: about 1 hour

Calories **245**
Protein **3g**
Cholesterol **10mg**
Total fat **7g**
Saturated fat **3g**
Sodium **110mg**

| | | |
|---|---|---|
| 125 g | plain flour | 4 oz |
| 2 tsp | caster sugar | 2 tsp |
| ¼ tsp | salt | ¼ tsp |
| 30 g | cold unsalted butter, cut into pieces | 1 oz |
| 15 g | cold unsalted polyunsaturated margarine, cut into pieces | ½ oz |
| ½ tsp | pure vanilla extract | ½ tsp |
| 300 g | cranberries, picked over | 10 oz |
| 4 tbsp | fresh orange juice | 4 tbsp |
| 5 tbsp | granulated sugar | 5 tbsp |
| 3 | ripe but firm pears, peeled, cored, cut into 5 mm (¼ inch) thick slices and tossed with the juice of ½ lemon | 3 |
| 1 tbsp | chopped hazelnuts (optional) | 1 tbsp |

To prepare the flan pastry, combine the flour, caster sugar and salt in a food processor or a bowl. If you are using a food processor, add the butter and margarine and cut them into the dry ingredients with several short bursts. With the motor running, slowly pour in the vanilla extract and 3 tablespoons of cold water, blending the dough just until it begins to form a ball. If you are making the dough in a bowl, use a pastry blender or two knives to cut the butter and margarine into the dry ingredients, then mix in the vanilla extract and water with a wooden spoon or your hands. Shape the dough into a ball and wrap it in plastic film. Chill the dough until it is firm enough to roll — about 20 minutes.

## BUFFET BRUNCH

*Pork Loin with Apple Juice and Rosemary*
*Scrambled Eggs with Smoked Salmon in Toast Cups*
*Wholemeal Scones with Burghul and Citrus*
*Pear Butter (recipe, page 49)*
*Pancake Torte with Spinach and Onion Filling*
*Broccoli Gratin*
*Riesling-Simmered Apricots and Pears*
*with Yogurt Cream*

Make the pear butter *(recipe, page 49)* for this buffet brunch up to a week in advance. The pancakes can be made a day or two ahead. The day before the brunch, cook the pork, and reduce the sauce to a glaze. Make the dessert and refrigerate it. Store everything in the refrigerator, well covered.

On the day of the brunch, make the broccoli gratin; the gratin can sit for up to 1 hour, covered, after it is baked. Bring the dessert and the meat to room temperature. Make and chill the dessert topping and bake the scones. Make the spinach-onion filling and fill the pancake; cover it with foil and then heat it in a 180°C (350°F or Mark 4) oven for about 5 minutes. Cook the swede and put it on a warmed platter; arrange the sliced meat on the swede, cover the platter with foil, and heat it in the oven with the pancake for about 10 minutes. Warm the glaze. If you like, heat the dessert for 15 minutes at 100°C (200°F or Mark ¼) to warm it.

# Pork Loin with Apple Juice and Rosemary

Serves 12
Working (and total) time: about 75 minutes

Calories **310**
Protein **32g**
Cholesterol **105mg**
Total fat **13g**
Saturated fat **3g**
Sodium **155mg**

| | | |
|---|---|---|
| 1 tbsp | safflower oil | 1 tbsp |
| 2 kg | boneless pork loin joint, trimmed of fat, cut into two pieces | 4 lb |
| 1 | small onion, coarsely chopped | 1 |
| 1½ tbsp | fresh rosemary, or 1 tsp dried rosemary | 1½ tbsp |
| ¼ tsp | salt | ¼ tsp |
| | freshly ground black pepper | |
| 1 litre | unsweetened apple juice | 1¾ pints |
| 3 tbsp | cider vinegar | 3 tbsp |
| 1 kg | swede, peeled and coarsely grated | 2 lb |
| 3 | fresh rosemary sprigs for garnish (optional) | 3 |

Heat the oil in a large, heavy frying pan over medium-high heat. Put the pork in the pan and brown it lightly on all sides — about 7 minutes in all. Add the onion, rosemary, salt and some pepper to the pan, pour in the apple juice and bring the mixture to the boil. Reduce the heat to medium low, cover the pan with the lid ajar, and simmer the pork for 25 minutes. Turn the meat pieces over and continue simmering them, partially covered, until the juices run clear when the meat is pierced with the tip of a sharp knife —about 20 minutes more. Remove the pork from the pan and keep it warm.

Add the vinegar to the pan and simmer the cooking liquid over medium-high heat until it is reduced to about 15 cl (¼ pint) — 15 to 20 minutes.

While the sauce is reducing, pour enough water into

a large saucepan to fill it about 2.5 cm (1 inch) deep. Set a vegetable steamer in the pan and put the swede into it. Cover the pan, bring the water to the boil, and steam the swede until it is tender — about 3 minutes. Drain the swede, pressing it lightly with the back of a spoon to release any excess liquid. Transfer the swede to a large serving platter and keep it warm.

Cut the pork into 3 mm (⅛ inch) thick slices and arrange the slices on top of the swede. Strain the sauce over the pork slices and, if you like, garnish the platter with the rosemary sprigs. Serve at once.

*A loaded sideboard awaits guests: pork loin on a bed of swede is served with squares of broccoli gratin, wedges of spinach-filled pancake torte, wholemeal scones with pear butter, scrambled eggs with salmon in toast-and-lettuce cups and, for dessert, Riesling-simmered apricots and pears.*

# Scrambled Eggs with Smoked Salmon in Toast Cups

CUTTING DOWN ON THE NUMBER OF EGG YOLKS USED
REDUCES THE CHOLESTEROL IN THIS RECIPE.

Serves 12
Working (and total) time: about 30 minutes

Calories **115**
Protein **7g**
Cholesterol **70mg**
Total fat **5g**
Saturated fat **1g**
Sodium **235mg**

| | | |
|---|---|---|
| 1 | round lettuce, or 150 g (5 oz) radicchio | 1 |
| 12 | slices wholemeal bread, crusts removed | 12 |
| 3 | whole eggs | 3 |
| 6 | egg whites | 6 |
| ⅛ tsp | salt | ⅛ tsp |
| | freshly ground black pepper | |
| 2 tbsp | virgin olive oil | 2 tbsp |
| 2 | garlic cloves, finely chopped | 2 |
| 125 g | sweet red pepper, seeded, deribbed and diced | 4 oz |
| 60 g | smoked salmon, finely chopped | 2 oz |
| 5 | spring onions, trimmed and thinly sliced | 5 |
| 1 tbsp | fresh lemon juice | 1 tbsp |

Separate the lettuce or radicchio leaves and wash them if necessary. Set the leaves aside. Preheat the oven to 200°C (400°F or Mark 6) and lightly oil 12 individual 7.5 cm (3 inch) fluted flan tins.

Using a rolling pin, flatten each slice of bread slightly. Gently press one slice of bread into each flan tin. Bake the bread until it is crisp and lightly browned — 10 to 15 minutes. Keep the toast cups warm.

Whisk together the eggs, egg whites, salt, some pepper and 1½ tablespoons of the oil in a large bowl. Heat the remaining ½ tablespoon of oil in a large, non-stick frying pan over medium-high heat. Add the garlic and red pepper and cook them for 1 minute, stirring constantly. Add the salmon, spring onions and lemon juice; cook the mixture for 2 minutes more. Pour in the egg mixture and cook it, stirring constantly, just until the eggs are set but still moist — about 2 minutes.

Spoon the scrambled eggs into the toast cups, place each toast cup on a lettuce leaf, and serve at once.

# Wholemeal Scones with Burghul and Citrus

Makes 16 scones
Working time: about 25 minutes
Total time: about 40 minutes

Per scone:
Calories **80**
Protein **3g**
Cholesterol **1mg**
Total fat **2g**
Saturated fat **0g**
Sodium **65mg**

| | | |
|---|---|---|
| 45 g | burghul | 1½ oz |
| ¼ litre | plain low-fat yogurt | 8 fl oz |
| 2 tsp | grated orange rind | 2 tsp |
| 1 tsp | grated lemon rind | 1 tsp |
| 2 tbsp | safflower oil | 2 tbsp |
| 175 g | wholemeal flour | 6 oz |
| 3 tbsp | sugar | 3 tbsp |
| 1½ tsp | baking powder | 1½ tsp |
| ⅛ tsp | salt | ⅛ tsp |

Put the burghul into a bowl and pour in 8 cl (3 fl oz) of boiling water. Cover the bowl and let the burghul stand until it is tender — about 15 minutes.

Preheat the oven to 190°C (375°F or Mark 5). Lightly oil a baking sheet or line it with parchment paper.

Drain the burghul thoroughly, put it into a large bowl, and stir in the yogurt, orange rind, lemon rind and oil. Sift the flour, sugar, baking powder and salt over the burghul mixture and stir them together just until they are combined. The dough will be quite sticky.

Turn the dough out on to a heavily floured surface. Dust your hands and the top of the dough with flour. Flatten the dough with your hands until it is about 5 mm (¼ inch) thick, using flour as needed to keep the dough from sticking. Using a 6 cm (2½ inch) round biscuit cutter, cut out as many scones as possible and put them on the baking sheet. Press the scraps of dough together and use them to make more scones.

Bake the scones until they are lightly browned — 15 to 20 minutes. Serve the scones hot.

# Pancake Torte with Spinach and Onion Filling

Serves 12
Working (and total) time: about 25 minutes

Calories **90**
Protein **4g**
Cholesterol **25mg**
Total fat **4g**
Saturated fat **1g**
Sodium **105mg**

| | | |
|---|---|---|
| 1 kg | fresh spinach, stemmed and washed, or 600 g (1¼ lb) frozen spinach, thawed | 2 lb |
| 2 tsp | virgin olive oil | 2 tsp |
| 2 | onions, thinly sliced | 2 |
| 1 tbsp | fresh thyme, or 1 tsp dried thyme | 1 tbsp |
| ⅛ tsp | salt | ⅛ tsp |
| | freshly ground black pepper | |
| 6 tbsp | cider vinegar | 6 tbsp |
| **Pancake batter** | | |
| 125 g | plain flour | 4 oz |
| ⅛ tsp | salt | ⅛ tsp |
| 30 cl | semi-skimmed milk | ½ pint |
| 1 | egg, plus 1 egg white | 1 |
| 1½ tbsp | virgin olive oil | 1½ tbsp |

To make the pancake batter, sift the flour and salt into a large bowl. In another bowl, whisk the milk, egg, egg white and oil together. Pour the milk mixture into the dry ingredients, stirring just until the batter is blended; do not overmix. Set the batter aside while you make the filling.

If you are using fresh spinach, cook it in 3 litres (5 pints) of boiling water for 1 minute, then drain it and run cold water over the spinach to refresh it; thawed frozen spinach does not require cooking. Squeeze the spinach in your hands to extract as much water as possible and coarsely chop it.

Heat the oil in a large, heavy frying pan over medium

heat. Add the onions, thyme, salt and some pepper, and cook the mixture, stirring occasionally, until the onions are translucent — about 10 minutes. Increase the heat to medium high and continue cooking, stirring frequently, until the onions have browned — 5 to 10 minutes more. Pour in the vinegar and continue to cook the onions until all the vinegar has evaporated — 1 to 2 minutes. Stir the spinach into the onions and cook the mixture for 1 minute. Keep the spinach mixture warm while you cook the pancakes.

Heat a 20 cm (8 inch) frying pan or griddle *(box, page 55)* over medium heat. Pour in half of the pancake batter and swirl the pan or griddle to distribute the batter over the bottom. Cook the pancake until the underside is golden — 2 to 3 minutes. Turn the pancake and cook it until the second side is browned — 2 to 3 minutes more. Transfer the pancake to a plate and keep it warm while you make a second pancake with the remaining batter.

Spread the spinach filling over the first pancake and top it with the second. Cut the pancake torte into 12 wedges and serve warm or at room temperature.

EDITOR'S NOTE: *The pancakes for this torte can be made up to two days in advance and kept in the refrigerator, covered with plastic film. On the day of the brunch, make the filling and spread it between the pancakes. Cover the torte with foil and heat it in a 180°C (350°F or Mark 4) oven for about 5 minutes.*

# Broccoli Gratin

Serves 12
Working time: about 25 minutes
Total time: about 1 hour and 15 minutes

Calories **75**
Protein **6g**
Cholesterol **35mg**
Total fat **4g**
Saturated fat **2g**
Sodium **135mg**

| | | |
|---|---|---|
| 1 kg | broccoli, the florets separated from the stems, the stems peeled and cut into 1 cm (½ inch) pieces | 2 lb |
| 12.5 cl | semi-skimmed milk | 4 fl oz |
| 250 g | low-fat ricotta cheese | 8 oz |
| 4 tbsp | single cream | 4 tbsp |
| 1 | egg, plus 1 egg white | 1 |
| 30 g | Parmesan cheese, freshly grated | 1 oz |
| 2 | garlic cloves, finely chopped | 2 |
| ¼ tsp | grated nutmeg | ¼ tsp |
| ¼ tsp | salt | ¼ tsp |
| | freshly ground black pepper | |

Preheat the oven to 180°C (350°F or Mark 4).

Pour enough water into a large saucepan to fill it about 2.5 cm (1 inch) deep. Set a vegetable steamer in the pan, bring the water to the boil, and put the broccoli stems into the steamer; cover the pan and steam the stems for 3 minutes. Add the broccoli florets and steam the florets and stems until both are tender — about 5 minutes more. Remove the steamer from the saucepan and refresh the broccoli under cold running water; drain it thoroughly.

Put the broccoli into a food processor and pour in the milk; process the broccoli in short bursts until it is coarsely puréed. (Do not overprocess — the mixture should not be smooth.)

In a large bowl, whisk together the ricotta, cream, egg, egg white, half of the Parmesan cheese, the garlic, nutmeg, salt and some pepper. Mix the broccoli purée into the ricotta mixture.

Spoon the broccoli mixture into a 20 by 30 cm (8 by 12 inch) baking dish; sprinkle it with the remaining Parmesan cheese. Bake the broccoli gratin in the oven until it is firm and lightly browned — 35 to 40 minutes. Cut the gratin into 12 squares or diamonds, arrange them on a large plate and serve.

# Riesling-Simmered Apricots and Pears with Yogurt Cream

Serves 12
Working time: about 30 minutes
Total time: about 1 hour and 15 minutes
(includes chilling)

Calories **130**
Protein **2g**
Cholesterol **10mg**
Total fat **3g**
Saturated fat **2g**
Sodium **10mg**

| | | |
|---|---|---|
| 35 cl | Riesling or other dry white wine | 12 fl oz |
| 350 g | dried apricots | 12 oz |
| 600 g | ripe pears, peeled, cored and cut into 2 cm (¾ inch) pieces | 1¼ lb |
| | **Yogurt cream** | |
| 6 tbsp | double cream | 6 tbsp |
| 4 tbsp | plain low-fat yogurt | 4 tbsp |
| 1 tbsp | icing sugar | 1 tbsp |
| 1 tsp | pure vanilla extract | 1 tsp |

Combine the wine and apricots in a large, non-reactive saucepan and bring the wine to a simmer over low heat. Simmer the mixture, stirring occasionally, until the apricots are soft and the liquid is reduced to about 12.5 cl (4 fl oz) — about 15 minutes.

Drain the apricots in a sieve set over a bowl, gently pressing them with a spoon to extract as much liquid as possible. Transfer the apricots to another bowl and set them aside. Pour the liquid back into the saucepan, add the pears, and cook them over low heat, stirring occasionally, until they are soft — about 20 minutes. The liquid should be syrupy. Line a 20 cm (8 inch) cake tin with a round of greaseproof paper or parchment paper.

Add the pears with their liquid to the apricots and gently stir them together. Arrange the apricots and pears in the prepared tin and spread them evenly over the bottom. Chill the fruit until it is firm — about 45 minutes.

Meanwhile, beat the cream until it forms soft peaks; mix in the yogurt, sugar and vanilla just until blended. Spoon the yogurt cream into a bowl and chill.

When the dish is set, run a knife round the edge of the tin and invert a serving plate on top of it. Turn both over together; lift away the pan and peel off the paper. Serve the dessert chilled or at room temperature topped with the yogurt cream.

# Techniques

## Shaping Pot Stickers

**1** *MOISTENING THE WRAPPER. Lay a dumpling wrapper on the work surface; keep the other wrappers under cloth or in their container to prevent dehydration. Place a heaped teaspoon of filling on the wrapper. Moisten a fingertip and run it along half of the wrapper's rim.*

**2** *PLEATING THE RIM. Pick up the wrapper with its filling and pinch the top of the moistened and unmoistened rims together. Then gather two or three pleats on each side of the dumpling and press to seal the edge.*

**3** *CURLING THE CRESCENT. To give a sharper crescent shape to the pot sticker, curl back its ends and pinch them between your fingers, as shown. Set the pot sticker aside on a lightly floured surface, covered with a damp cloth, and form the other pot stickers in the same manner.*

## Forming Buns

**1** *FILLING THE BUN. After making the dough rounds as directed in the recipe on page 98, set one before you on the work surface. Place a heaped teaspoon of the prepared bean filling on to the centre of the round.*

**2** *SHAPING THE BUN. Pick up the round and its filling and gather up the sides with your fingers. Enclose the filling by simultaneously pinching and twisting the edges together. Set the bun aside and fill and form the other buns in the same manner.*

## Preparing Artichokes for Summer Salad with Fresh Tuna

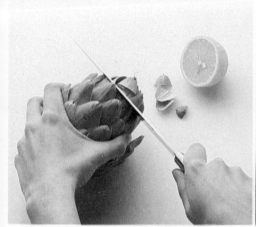 

**1** TRIMMING THE TOP. With a stainless-steel knife, cut off about 2.5 cm (1 inch) of the top of an artichoke. To prevent discoloration, rub the trimmed edges with a freshly cut lemon.

**2** SNIPPING THE LEAF TIPS. Trim off the hard, prickly tips of the outer leaves with kitchen scissors. Use the knife to cut off the stem of the artichoke near the base of the globe. Rub the trimmed edges with lemon. Repeat Steps 1 and 2 with the other artichoke. Cook and cool the artichokes as directed in the recipe. Slice them in half lengthwise.

**3** REMOVING THE CHOKE. Hold a half in the palm of one hand and use a small, sturdy spoon to dig out the choke — the inedible, furry centre. Discard the choke and slice the half into thirds for the salad. Repeat the procedures for the other three halves.

## Carving Cucumber Boats

**1** CARVING THE PEEL. With a sharp knife, cut off the ends of a cucumber. Holding the cucumber firmly in one hand, use a canelle knife (shown here) or vegetable peeler to score the peel lengthwise at intervals of about 1 cm (½ inch).

**2** MAKING BOATS. Cut the cucumber in half lengthwise. With a small, sturdy spoon, scoop out the seeds, leaving about 5 mm (¼ inch) of flesh on the sides and a thicker base. Divide each cucumber half into three equal segments.

*3* *Brown bread with walnuts and apricots takes only 8 minutes to bake in the microwave oven (recipe, opposite page).*

# Microwaved Breakfasts

The microwave truly comes into its own in the morning, when the minutes that it shaves from conventional cooking times are especially important to the hurried cook. Seven of the recipes in this section constitute a selection of quick and easy breakfast and brunch dishes — breads; fruit and vegetable dishes; and bran muffins that can be prepared, from start to finish, in just 10 minutes. And as a bonus, there are two recipes for preserves that can help brighten up a breakfast; they cannot be beaten for colour and freshness, but unlike ordinary jams and jellies, these have to be stored in the refrigerator. Most of the recipes in this section require less than half an hour overall time, and in no instance does the necessary working time exceed 30 minutes.

The abbreviated cooking process offers a number of advantages in addition to convenience. Not only does microwaving help preserve natural colour, shape and texture; it also ensures that fewer nutrients are destroyed. And when fruits and vegetables are cooked in the microwave oven, they essentially cook in their own juices, with only a little additional liquid needed. As a result, fewer of the heat-sensitive and water-soluble vitamins and minerals are destroyed or drawn out of the food.

The microwave process cannot brown the surface of breads and biscuits: they generally emerge from the oven looking unappealingly pallid when white flour is used. Thus whole-grain products are called for here; the brown bread on the left and the raisin and nut spreads on page 137 owe their appetizing appearance to well-chosen ingredients, which also have the advantage of furnishing fibre, vitamins, minerals and protein appropriate to a healthy morning meal.

All of the recipes have been tested in both 625-watt and 700-watt ovens. Since power settings often vary among ovens made by different manufacturers, the recipes use "high" to indicate 100 per cent power, "medium high" for 70 per cent and "medium low" for 30 per cent.

## Brown Bread with Walnuts and Apricots

Serves 10
Working time: about 15 minutes
Total time: about 30 minutes

Calories **155**
Protein **4g**
Cholesterol **0mg**
Total fat **2g**
Saturated fat **0g**
Sodium **160mg**

| | | |
|---|---|---|
| 60 g | dried apricots | 2 oz |
| 12.5 cl | buttermilk | 4 fl oz |
| 175 g | molasses | 6 oz |
| 1 | egg white | 1 |
| 125 g | wholemeal flour | 4 oz |
| 60 g | cornmeal | 2 oz |
| 2 tbsp | dark brown sugar | 2 tbsp |
| ¼ tsp | salt | ¼ tsp |
| 1 tsp | bicarbonate of soda | 1 tsp |
| 30 g | shelled walnuts, chopped | 1 oz |

Put the apricots into a glass measuring jug and pour in 4 tablespoons of water. Microwave the apricots on high for 2 minutes.

In a bowl, mix together the apricots, buttermilk, molasses and egg white. In another bowl, stir together the flour, cornmeal, brown sugar, salt, bicarbonate of soda and walnuts. Stir the flour mixture into the apricots to combine them.

Lightly oil a 23 by 10 cm (9 by 4 inch) glass loaf dish and spoon in the batter. Put a glass pie plate upside down in the microwave oven; set the loaf dish on it. (This is not recommended for ovens with rotating turntables.) Microwave the loaf on medium (50 per cent power) for 8 minutes, rotating the dish a quarter turn every 2 minutes. If areas of the bread start to overcook, shield them with small pieces of aluminium foil. Check the bread for doneness by inserting a wooden pick or a skewer into the centre; if it comes out clean, the bread is done. Set the loaf dish on a rack and let the bread cool in the dish for 10 minutes before unmoulding and slicing it.

# Prunes with Orange, Pineapple and Kiwi Fruit

Serves 6
Working (and total) time: about 30 minutes

Calories **90**
Protein **1g**
Cholesterol **0mg**
Total fat **0g**
Saturated fat **0g**
Sodium **2mg**

| | | |
|---|---|---|
| 500 g | dried stoned prunes, quartered | 1 lb |
| 1½ tsp | cornflour | 1½ tsp |
| 6 tbsp | fresh orange juice | 6 tbsp |
| 3 tbsp | honey | 3 tbsp |
| ½ tsp | pure vanilla extract | ½ tsp |
| 1 | orange | 1 |
| 150 g | fresh pineapple, cut into 2.5 cm (1 inch) wedges | 5 oz |
| 1 | kiwi fruit, halved and cut into 12 pieces (six pieces per half) | 1 |

Put the prunes and 60 cl (1 pint) of hot water into a bowl. Cover the bowl and microwave it on high until the water simmers — about 4 minutes. Remove the bowl from the oven and let the prunes stand, covered, for about 10 minutes.

Meanwhile, combine the cornflour and the fresh orange juice in a bowl, then stir in the honey and the vanilla extract. Cook the mixture on high until it thickens — about 2 minutes.

Using a sharp, stainless-steel knife, cut off both ends of the orange. Stand the orange on end and cut away vertical strips of the peel and pith. Slice the orange into 5 mm (¼ inch) thick rounds. Cut the rounds in half.

Drain the prunes and put them into a bowl with the orange, pineapple and kiwi fruit. Pour the honey mixture over the fruits and stir them together gently. Microwave the fruit mixture on high for 1½ minutes to heat it through. Serve the fruit warm.

# Bran Muffins with Dates

Makes 6 muffins
Working time: about 5 minutes
Total time: about 10 minutes

Per muffin:
Calories **205**
Protein **5g**
Cholesterol **2mg**
Total fat **4g**
Saturated fat **1g**
Sodium **240mg**

| | | |
|---|---|---|
| 90 g | stoned dried dates, chopped | 3 oz |
| 50 g | plain flour | 1¾ oz |
| 60 g | wholemeal flour | 2 oz |
| 30 g | wheat bran | 1 oz |
| ⅛ tsp | salt | ⅛ tsp |
| ¾ tsp | bicarbonate of soda | ¾ tsp |
| ¼ litre | plain low-fat yogurt | 8 fl oz |
| 90 g | molasses | 3 oz |
| 4 tsp | safflower oil | 4 tsp |

Mix the dates with 1 teaspoon of the plain flour and reserve them. Combine the remaining plain flour, the wholemeal flour, bran, salt and bicarbonate of soda in a bowl. Add the yogurt, molasses and oil, and stir gently until all of these ingredients are combined. Fold the dates into the batter.

Line the cups of a microwave deep bun pan with paper cake cases or lightly oil six 12.5 cl (4 fl oz) ramekins. Divide the batter among the cups or ramekins. Cook the muffins on high for about 3 minutes, turning the pan or rearranging the ramekins half way through the cooking time. Test the muffins for doneness every 30 seconds by inserting a wooden toothpick in their centres; when the pick comes out clean, remove the muffins from the oven. Let the muffins stand for 5 minutes before serving them.

# Spiced Fig Cake
# with Chutney Sauce

Serves 10
Working time: about 15 minutes
Total time: about 35 minutes

Calories **150**
Protein **3g**
Cholesterol **1mg**
Total fat **3g**
Saturated fat **0g**
Sodium **160mg**

| | | |
|---|---|---|
| 225 g | plain flour | 7½ oz |
| 4 tbsp | caster sugar | 4 tbsp |
| 2 tsp | baking powder | 2 tsp |
| 1 tsp | curry powder | 1 tsp |
| ¼ tsp | salt | ¼ tsp |
| 15 cl | skimmed milk | ¼ pint |
| 2 tbsp | safflower oil | 2 tbsp |
| 1 | egg white | 1 |
| 90 g | dried figs, coarsely chopped | 3 oz |
| 1 | lemon, grated rind only | 1 |
| **Chutney sauce** | | |
| ½ tbsp | cornflour | ½ tbsp |
| 17.5 cl | unsweetened apple juice | 6 fl oz |
| 2 tbsp | mango chutney | 2 tbsp |
| 40 g | sultanas | 1¼ oz |

Combine the flour, sugar, baking powder, curry powder and salt in a bowl. Add the milk, oil and egg white to the dry ingredients and stir them together just until blended. Gently mix in the figs and the lemon rind.

Lightly oil a 1.25 litre (2 pint) glass or plastic ring mould. Spoon the cake batter evenly into the mould, smoothing the top of the batter with the back of the spoon. Tap the mould several times on the worktop to release any air bubbles from the batter.

Microwave the cake on medium high (70 per cent power) for about 8 minutes, rotating the cake a third of a turn twice during the cooking time. When the cake is done, a wooden toothpick or a skewer inserted into the centre will come out clean. Remove the cake from the oven and let it cool.

While the cake cools, combine the cornflour and apple juice in a small bowl and stir the mixture to dissolve the cornflour. Add the chutney and sultanas and microwave the mixture on high until the sauce has thickened — about 2 minutes. Remove the sauce from the oven, stir it, and let it stand until cool.

Unmould the cake on to a serving plate, slice it, and serve with the sauce.

# Seedless Cranberry Jam

Makes 600 g (1¼ lb)
Working time: about 10 minutes
Total time: about 8 hours (includes chilling)

| | | |
|---|---|---|
| 350 g | cranberries, picked over | 12 oz |
| 150 g | sugar | 5 oz |
| 1 tbsp | liquid pectin | 1 tbsp |

Per tablespoon:
Calories **25**
Protein **0g**
Cholesterol **0mg**
Total fat **0g**
Saturated fat **0g**
Sodium **0mg**

Put the cranberries into a 2 litre (3½ pint) glass bowl with ¼ litre (8 fl oz) of water and microwave them on high, uncovered, for 6 minutes.

Work the cranberries through a sieve set over a bowl and discard the contents of the sieve. Add the sugar to the bowl and stir the mixture. Microwave the cranberry mixture on high for 8 minutes, stirring half way through the cooking time. Remove the bowl from the oven, stir in the pectin, and let the jam cool.

Spoon the jam into a jar, and cover and chill it overnight. Cranberry jam can be kept for up to 2 weeks covered and stored in the refrigerator.

# Tangerine Marmalade

Makes 250 g (8 oz)
Working time: about 10 minutes
Total time: about 2 hours and 30 minutes
(includes cooling)

| | | |
|---|---|---|
| 250 g | tangerines (about three) | 8 oz |
| ⅛ tsp | pure vanilla extract | ⅛ tsp |
| 150 g | sugar | 5 oz |

Per tablespoon:
Calories **55**
Protein **0g**
Cholesterol **0mg**
Total fat **0g**
Saturated fat **0g**
Sodium **0mg**

Remove the peel from the tangerines and chop it finely. Put the chopped peel into a measuring jug. Squeeze the tangerines and strain the juice into the measuring jug; add the vanilla extract and stir well. If necessary, add enough water to measure ¼ litre (8 fl oz).

Pour the tangerine mixture into a bowl and microwave it, uncovered, on high for 5 minutes. Stir in the sugar and microwave the bowl on high for 5 minutes more. Stir the mixture and then microwave it for 3 minutes more. Test the marmalade for consistency by dropping a spoonful of it on to a chilled plate (right). Let the marmalade cool for 1 minute and then push it gently with your finger tip; it should wrinkle slightly as you push it. If the marmalade fails to wrinkle, microwave it for up to 1 minute more and then test it again; but be very careful not to overcook the marmalade or it will become too thick.

Let the marmalade cool to room temperature before serving it — about 2 hours. The marmalade can be stored in the refrigerator for up to two weeks.

EDITOR'S NOTE: If the marmalade thickens too much during refrigeration, you can thin it by microwaving it, uncovered, on high for 1 minute. Stir in 2 tablespoons of water and microwave it on high for 2 minutes more; then allow it to cool.

## Obtaining a Proper Set

TESTING THE MARMALADE. Drop a spoonful of the marmalade on to a flat plate that has been well chilled. Let the syrup cool for 1 minute, then slowly push a finger across it. If done, the marmalade should wrinkle slightly. If not, microwave the syrup for another minute and then test again.

# Pork and Spinach Pie

Serves 6 as a main course
Working time: about 30 minutes
Total time: about 1 hour

Calories **300**
Protein **22g**
Cholesterol **85mg**
Total fat **11g**
Saturated fat **4g**
Sodium **570mg**

| 300 g | frozen chopped spinach | 10 oz |
|---|---|---|
| 250 g | pork fillet, trimmed of fat and finely chopped | 8 oz |
| 1 tsp | fennel seeds | 1 tsp |
| 2 | garlic cloves, finely chopped | 2 |
| 1 tsp | ground coriander | 1 tsp |
| ⅛ tsp | salt | ⅛ tsp |
| 1 tbsp | virgin olive oil | 1 tbsp |
| ½ tsp | dried hot red pepper flakes | ½ tsp |
| 60 cl | buttermilk | 1 pint |
| 1 | egg, plus 1 egg white | 1 |
| 1 | loaf French bread (about 250 g/8 oz), cut into 1 cm (½ inch) thick slices | 1 |
| 60 g | Parmesan cheese, freshly grated | 2 oz |

To thaw the frozen spinach, set it in its packet on a plate and microwave the spinach on high for 2½ minutes. Set the spinach aside.

In a bowl, mix together the pork, fennel seeds, garlic, coriander, salt, ½ tablespoon of the oil and ¼ teaspoon of the red pepper flakes. In another bowl, mix the buttermilk, egg and egg white, the remaining oil

and the remaining red pepper flakes.

Spread the bread slices in a single layer on the bottom of a shallow baking tray. Pour all but 4 tablespoons of the buttermilk mixture over the bread, then turn the slices. Let the bread stand, turning the slices frequently until they have absorbed nearly all the liquid — about 15 minutes.

Microwave the pork mixture on high for 1½ minutes, stirring the mixture once at midpoint. Remove the spinach from the package and squeeze it with your hands to remove as much liquid as possible. Stir the spinach into the pork mixture, along with the reserved 4 tablespoons of the buttermilk mixture and about half of the cheese.

Spoon about a quarter of the pork mixture into a 28 cm (11 inch) glass pie plate. Arrange half of the bread slices in a close-fitting layer on top of the pork. Cover the bread with half of the remaining pork mixture and top this layer with the remaining bread. Spread the remaining pork mixture on top of the bread and pour over any of the buttermilk mixture remaining on the baking tray. Cover the dish.

Microwave the dish on medium (50 per cent power) for 4 minutes. Rotate the dish half way and cook it for another 4 minutes. Uncover the dish and scatter the remaining cheese over the top. Cook the dish 8 minutes more. Let the dish stand for at least 5 minutes before serving it.

# Spaghetti Squash
# with Basil and Pine-Nuts

Serves 6
Working time: about 10 minutes
Total time: about 40 minutes

Calories **105**
Protein **3g**
Cholesterol **1mg**
Total fat **3g**
Saturated fat **0g**
Sodium **80mg**

| | | |
|---|---|---|
| 1 | spaghetti squash (about 2 kg/4 lb) | 1 |
| 4 tbsp | unsalted chicken stock (recipe, page 138) or water | 4 tbsp |
| 1 | ripe tomato, skinned, seeded and cut into small dice | 1 |
| 4 tbsp | chopped fresh basil | 4 tbsp |
| 2 tbsp | pine-nuts, toasted in a small, dry frying pan over medium heat | 2 tbsp |
| 2 tbsp | freshly grated Parmesan cheese | 2 tbsp |
| 1 tsp | fresh lemon juice | 1 tsp |
| 1 tbsp | caster sugar | 1 tbsp |
| 1 | whole basil leaf for garnish (optional) | 1 |

Pierce the squash several times with the point of a sharp knife. Put the squash into a shallow casserole and microwave it on high for 20 minutes, turning it over half way through the cooking. Remove the squash from the oven and let it stand for 10 minutes.

Cut the squash in half lengthwise; remove and discard the seeds. Using a fork, remove the flesh of the squash and put it into a bowl. Add the stock or water, tomato, chopped basil, pine-nuts, Parmesan cheese, lemon juice and sugar and toss them all together. Microwave the mixture on high for 4 minutes. Remove the squash from the oven and let it cool slightly. Put the squash into a serving dish and garnish the dish with the basil leaf, if you are using it. Serve the squash at once.

# Chewy Sultana and Nut Squares

Makes 16 squares
Working time: about 15 minutes
Total time: about 30 minutes

Per square:
Calories **135**
Protein **3g**
Cholesterol **0mg**
Total fat **5g**
Saturated fat **0g**
Sodium **20mg**

| | | |
|---|---|---|
| 7 g | puffed wheat | ¼ oz |
| 100 g | rolled oats | 3½ oz |
| 4 tbsp | wheat germ | 4 tbsp |
| 12.5 cl | unsweetened apple juice | 4 fl oz |
| 2 | egg whites | 2 |
| 125 g | honey | 4 oz |
| 3 tbsp | safflower oil | 3 tbsp |
| ⅛ tsp | almond extract | ⅛ tsp |
| 60 g | wholemeal flour | 2 oz |
| ½ tsp | baking powder | ½ tsp |
| 30 g | shelled walnuts, chopped | 1 oz |
| 30 g | blanched almonds, chopped | 1 oz |
| 125 g | sultanas | 4 oz |

Combine the puffed wheat, rolled oats and wheat germ in a bowl and stir in the apple juice; set the mixture aside for 5 minutes to absorb the juice. Lightly oil a 20 cm (8 inch) square baking dish.

In another bowl, whisk together the egg whites, honey, oil and almond extract, then stir in the cereal mixture. Add the flour and baking powder and stir the batter just until they are mixed in. Fold in the walnuts, almonds and sultanas.

Spread the batter in the baking dish, smoothing the surface of the batter with the back of a spoon.

Microwave the cake on medium high (70 per cent power) for 6 minutes, rotating the dish a quarter turn every 2 minutes. If areas of the cake start to overcook, shield them with small pieces of aluminium foil. Discard the foil shields, if you are using them, and let the cake cool to room temperature. The cake will be quite moist and soft in the centre at first but it will get firmer as it cools. Cut the cake into 16 squares and serve it at room temperature. The squares can be stored for up to a week in an airtight container.

## Brown Stock

Makes about 3 litres (5 pints)
Working time: about 40 minutes
Total time: about 5½ hours

| 1.5 kg | veal breast (or veal or beef shin meat), cut into 7.5 cm (3 inch) pieces | 3 lb |
|---|---|---|
| 1.5 kg | uncooked veal or beef bones, cracked | 3 lb |
| 2 | onions, quartered | 2 |
| 2 | sticks celery, chopped | 2 |
| 2 | carrots, sliced | 2 |
| 3 | unpeeled garlic cloves, crushed | 3 |
| 8 | black peppercorns | 8 |
| 3 | cloves | 3 |
| 2 tsp | fresh thyme, or ½ tsp dried thyme | 2 tsp |
| 1 | bay leaf | 1 |

Preheat the oven to 220°C (425°F or Mark 7). Place the meat, bones, onions, celery and carrots in a large roasting pan and roast them in the oven until they are well browned — about 1 hour.

Transfer the contents of the roasting pan to a large saucepan. Pour ½ litre (16 fl oz) of water into the roasting pan; with a spatula, scrape up the browned bits from the bottom of the pan. Pour the liquid into the saucepan.

Add the garlic, peppercorns and cloves. Pour in enough water to cover the contents of the pan by about 7.5 cm (3 inches). Bring the liquid to the boil, then reduce the heat to maintain a simmer, and skim any impurities from the surface. Add the thyme and bay leaf, then simmer the stock very gently for 4 hours, skimming occasionally during the process.

Strain the stock; allow the solids to drain thoroughly into the stock before discarding them. Degrease the stock.

EDITOR'S NOTE: *Thoroughly browning the meat, bones and vegetables should produce a stock with a rich mahogany colour. If your stock does not seem dark enough, cook 1 tablespoon of tomato paste in a small pan over medium heat, stirring constantly, until it darkens — about 3 minutes. Add this to the stock about 1 hour before the end of the cooking time.*

*Any combination of meat and bones may be used to make the stock; ideally, the meat and bones together should weigh about 3 kg (6 lb). Ask your butcher to crack the bones.*

## Chicken Stock

Makes about 2 litres (3½ pints)
Working time: about 20 minutes
Total time: about 3 hours

| 2 to 2.5 kg | uncooked chicken trimmings and (preferably wings, necks and backs), the bones cracked with a heavy knife | 4 to 5 lb |
|---|---|---|
| 2 | carrots, cut into 1 cm (½ inch) thick rounds | 2 |
| 2 | sticks celery, cut into 2.5 cm (1 inch) pieces | 2 |
| 2 | large onions (about 500 g/1 lb), cut in half, one half stuck with 2 cloves | 2 |
| 2 | fresh thyme sprigs, or ½ tsp dried thyme | 2 |
| 1 or 2 | bay leaves | 1 or 2 |
| 10 to 15 | parsley stems | 10 to 15 |
| 5 | black peppercorns | 5 |

Put the chicken trimmings and bones into a heavy stockpot; pour in enough water to cover them by about 5 cm (2 inches). Bring the liquid to the boil over medium heat, skimming off the scum that rises to the surface. Reduce the heat and simmer the liquid for 10 minutes, skimming and adding a little cold water to help precipitate the scum.

Add the vegetables, herbs and peppercorns, and submerge them in the liquid. If necessary, pour in enough additional water to cover the contents of the pot. Simmer the stock for 2 to 3 hours, skimming as necessary to remove the scum.

Strain the stock into a bowl, discard the solids, and degrease the stock.

EDITOR'S NOTE: *The chicken gizzard and heart may be added to the stock. Wings and necks — rich in natural gelatine — produce a particularly gelatinous stock, ideal for sauces and jellied dishes.*

*Turkey, duck or goose stock may be prepared using the same basic recipe.*

# Glossary

**Al dente:** an Italian term meaning "to the tooth". It is used to describe the texture and taste of perfectly cooked pasta: chewy but with no taste of flour.

**Basil:** a fragrant herb with an underlying flavour of clove. If whole fresh basil leaves are covered with olive oil and refrigerated in a tightly sealed container, they may be kept for several months.

**Bâton** (also called bâtonnet): a vegetable piece that has been cut in the shape of a stick; bâtons are slightly larger than julienne.

**Buckwheat:** the seed of the flowering buckwheat plant. Although technically not a true cereal grain, buckwheat is ground into a flour used primarily to make pancakes. Buckwheat flour lacks the protein required to form gluten. See also Kasha.

**Burghul:** whole-wheat kernels that have been steamed, dried and cracked. Burghul can be found in health food shops and some supermarkets.

**Buttermilk:** a tangy, cultured-milk product that, despite its name, contains less than 1 per cent milk fat as opposed to the 3.3 per cent in whole milk. However, buttermilk often has about twice the sodium of whole milk.

**Calorie** (or kilocalorie): a precise measure of the energy food supplies when it is broken down for use in the body.

**Capers:** the pickled flower buds of the caper plant, a shrub native to the Mediterranean. Capers should be rinsed before use to rid them of excess salt.

**Caramelize:** to heat sugar, or a food naturally rich in sugar such as fruit, until the sugar turns brown and syrupy.

**Caraway seeds:** the pungent seed of the herb caraway, often used to flavour rye bread.

**Cardamom:** the bittersweet, aromatic dried seed pods of a plant in the ginger family. When removed from the pod, cardamom seeds may be used whole or ground.

**Cayenne pepper:** a fiery powder ground from the seeds and pods of various red chili peppers.

**Chicory:** a small, cigar-shaped vegetable, composed of many tightly wrapped white to pale yellow leaves.

**Chili peppers:** a variety of hot red or green peppers. Serranos and jalapeños are small fresh green chilies that are extremely hot. Anchos are dried poblano chilies that are mildly hot and dark red in colour. Fresh or dried, chili peppers contain volatile oils that can irritate the skin and eyes; they must be handled with extreme care (caution, page 103).

**Chinese cabbage** (also called Chinese leaves): an elongated cabbage resembling cos lettuce, with long broad ribs and crinkled, light green to white leaves.

**Cholesterol:** a waxlike substance that is manufactured in the human body and also found in foods of animal origin. Although a certain amount of cholesterol is necessary for proper body functioning, an excess can accumulate in the arteries, contributing to heart disease. See also Monounsaturated fats; Polyunsaturated fats; Saturated fats.

**Chutney:** a pickle of Indian origin that can be made of fruits, vegetables, spices, vinegar and sugar. It is served cooked or raw, traditionally with curry. The cooked variety is available bottled.

**Coriander** (also called cilantro): the pungent peppery leaves of the coriander plant or its earthy tasting dried seeds. It is a common seasoning in Middle-Eastern, Oriental and Latin-American cookery.

**Crêpe:** a paper thin pancake that can accommodate a variety of savoury or sweet fillings.

**Crystallized ginger** (also called candied ginger): the spicy, rootlike stems of ginger preserved dry with sugar. Crystallized ginger should not be confused with ginger in syrup; the two are not always interchangeable.

**Cumin:** the aromatic seeds of an umbelliferous plant similar to fennel used, whole or powdered, as a spice, especially in Indian and Latin-American dishes. Raw, the seeds add a pleasant bitterness to curry powder and chili powder; toasted, they have a nutty taste.

**Daikon radish** (also called mooli): long, white Japanese radish.

**Dijon mustard:** a smooth or grainy mustard once manufactured only in Dijon, France; may be flavoured with herbs, green peppercorns or white wine.

**Farina:** a white wheat flour used most commonly in Middle-Eastern desserts.

**Fennel:** a herb (also called wild fennel) whose feathery leaves and dried seeds have a mild anise flavour and are much used for flavouring. Its vegetable relative, the bulb — or Florence — fennel (also called finocchio) can be cooked, or eaten raw in salads.

**Filbert:** see Hazelnut.

**Fish sauce** (also called *nuoc mam* and *nam pla*): a thin, brown, salty liquid made from fermented fish and used in South-East Asian cooking to bring out the flavours of a dish.

**Frappé:** a chilled or partly frozen, frothy beverage.

**Fricassee:** a type of stew traditionally made with poultry and served in white sauce.

**Frittata:** an open-faced omelette.

**Gelatine:** a tasteless protein, available in powdered form or in sheets. Dissolved gelatine is used to firm liquid mixtures so that they can be moulded.

**Ginger:** the spicy, buff-coloured, rootlike stem of the ginger plant, used as a seasoning either fresh or dried and powdered. The dried form should never be substituted for the fresh. See also Crystallized ginger.

**Grouper:** a fish caught in temperate and tropical waters around the world, Its flesh is lean, moist and sweet. Depending on the species, groupers range in size from 500 g to 320 kg (1 to 700 lb).

**Gyoza wrappers:** round, moist wonton wrappers, made of wheat flour and eggs.

**Hazelnut:** the fruit of a shrublike tree. Filberts, which are cultivated, are found primarily in Turkey, Italy and Spain, and in the United States. They have a stronger flavour than hazelnuts, which grow wild. Both are prized by bakers and sweetmakers.

**Hot red pepper sauce:** a hot, unsweetened chili sauce, such as Tabasco.

**Julienne:** the French term for food cut into thin strips.

**Kasha:** toasted buckwheat groats.

**Kiwi fruit:** an egg-shaped fruit with a fuzzy brown skin, tart, lime green flesh and hundreds of tiny black edible seeds. Peeled and sliced, the kiwi displays a starburst of seeds at its centre that lends a decorative note to tarts and other desserts.

**Lefse:** a large, thin Norwegian potato pancake that is cooked on an ungreased griddle.

**Mace:** the ground aril, or covering, that encases the nutmeg seed, widely used as a flavouring agent in baking.

**Mackerel:** a rich-fleshed fish, weighing 500 g to 2 kg (1 to 4 lb). Mackerel's firm flesh, high in oil, flakes easily and lightens in colour when cooked.

**Mango:** a fruit grown throughout the tropics, with sweet, succulent, yellow-orange flesh that is extremely rich in vitamin A. Like papaya, it may cause an allergic reaction in some individuals.

**Meringue:** an airy concoction made from stiffly beaten egg whites and sugar. It serves as the base for mousses and soufflés; meringue may also be baked in biscuit form or as edible containers for desserts.

**Millet:** a nutritious grain with a nutty, mild taste. Millet flakes can be added to breakfast cereals.

**Monounsaturated fats:** one of the three types of fats found in foods. Monounsaturated fats are believed not to raise the level of cholesterol in the blood.

**Non-reactive pan:** a cooking vessel whose surface does not react chemically with the acids in food. Materials used include ovenproof clay, stainless steel, enamel, glass and aluminium that has been finished with a non-stick coating. Untreated cast iron and aluminium may react with acids, producing discoloration or a peculiar taste.

**Olive oil:** any of various grades of oil extracted from olives. Extra virgin olive oil has a full, fruity flavour and the lowest acidity. Virgin olive oil is slightly higher in acidity. Pure olive oil, a processed blend of olive oils, has the hightest acidity and the lightest taste.

**Papaya** (also called pawpaw): a pear-shaped, melon-like tropical fruit rich in vitamins A and C. Like mango, it may cause an allergic reaction in some individuals.

**Parchment paper:** a reusable paper treated with silicone to produce a non-stick surface. It is used to line cake tins and baking sheets, and to wrap foods for baking.

**Pear brandy:** a clear white spirit distilled from pears.

**Pectin:** a substance extracted from citrus fruits and apples and used to thicken jams and jellies. Some fruits, including most berries, are rich enough in pectin to gel on their own. Other fruits — peaches and strawberries, for example – are quite low in pectin, and need added pectin to gel.

**Phyllo** (also spelt "filo"): a paper-thin flour-and-water pastry popular in Greece and the Middle East. It can be made at home or bought, fresh or frozen, from delicatessens and shops specializing in Middle-Eastern food. Because frozen phyllo dries out easily, it should be thawed in the refrigerator, and any phyllo sheets not in use should be covered with a damp towel.

**Pine-nuts** (also called *pignoli*): seeds from the cone of the stone pine, a tree native to the Mediterranean. Toasting brings out their buttery flavour.

**Poach:** to cook a food in barely simmering liquid as a means of preserving moisture and adding flavour.

**Polyunsaturated fats:** one of the three types of fats found in foods. They exist in abundance in such vegetable oils as safflower, sunflower, corn and soya bean. Polyunsaturated fats lower the level of cholesterol in the blood.

**Pomegranate:** The succulent seeds of this red-skinned fruit are picked out and eaten; the bitter white membranes are discarded. Pomegranates are in season in the autumn.

**Purée:** to reduce food to a smooth, even, pulplike consistency by mashing it, passing it through a sieve, or processing it in a food processor or a blender.

**Recommended Daily Amount (RDA):** the average daily amount of an essential nutrient recommended for healthy people by the U.K. Department of Health and Social Security.

**Reduce:** to boil down a liquid or sauce in order to concentrate its flavour or thicken its consistency.

**Refresh:** to rinse a briefly cooked vegetable under cold running water to arrest its cooking and set its colour.

**Rice vinegar:** a mild, fragrant vinegar that is less sweet than cider vinegar and not as harsh as distilled white vinegar. It is available in dark, light, seasoned and sweetened varieties; Japanese rice vinegar generally is milder than the Chinese version.

**Rice wine:** wine made from fermented rice. The best imported Chinese rice wine is shao-hsing, but it is difficult to find outside Asian communities. Japanese rice wine, sake, has a different flavour, but it may be used as a substitute for the Chinese variety. If rice wine is unavailable, use dry sherry.

**Rind:** the flavourful outermost layer of citrus fruit peel; it should be cut or grated free of the white pith that lies beneath it.

**Rolled oats:** a cereal made from oats that have been ground into meal, then steamed, rolled into flakes and dried.

**Rye:** an ancient grain, which grows well under poor conditions. Rye is a popular bread flour in Northern Europe; it yields a dense loaf because of its low protein content.

**Safflower oil:** a vegetable oil that contains the highest proportion of polyunsaturated fats.

**Saffron:** the dried, yellowish-red stigmas (or threads) of the saffron crocus, which yield a powerful yellow colour as well as a pungent flavour. Powdered saffron may be substituted for the threads but has less flavour.

**Salsa:** an accompaniment to many Mexican dishes, salsa is a fiery condiment made from chili peppers.

**Saturated fats:** one of the three types of fats found in food. They exist in abundance in animal products and coconut and palm oils; they raise the level of cholesterol in the blood. Because high blood-cholesterol levels may cause heart disease, saturated fat consumption should be restricted to less than 15 per cent of the calories provided by the daily diet.

**Scallop:** a bivalve mollusc found throughout the world, in the Atlantic from Iceland to Spain and in the Pacific from Alaska to Australia. The white nut of meat (actually the adductor muscle) and the orange roe, or coral, are eaten. Tiny queen scallops are a different species from the familiar larger scallops known in France as *coquilles Saint-Jacques*.

**Shallot:** a mild variety of onion, with a subtle flavour and papery, red-brown skin.

**Sherry vinegar:** a full-bodied vinegar made from sherry; its distinguishing feature is a sweet aftertaste.

**Simmer:** to heat a liquid or sauce to just below its boiling point, so that the liquid's surface barely trembles.

**Sodium:** a nutrient essential to maintaining the proper balance of fluids in the body. In most diets, a major source of the element is table salt, which contains 40 per cent sodium. Excess sodium may contribute to high blood pressure, which increases the risk of heart disease. One teaspoon (5.5 g) of salt, with 2,132 milligrams of sodium, contains just over the maximum daily amount recommended by the World Health Organization.

**Sorbet:** a frozen mixture of fruit or vegetable purée or juice, sugar and often water that may be served as a dessert or as a refreshing interlude between courses.

**Soy sauce:** a savoury, salty brown liquid made from fermented soya beans. One tablespoon of ordinary soy sauce contains 1,030 milligrams of sodium; lower-sodium variations, such as naturally fermented shoyu, used in the recipes in this book, may contain as little as half that amount.

**Spaghetti squash:** a yellow-skinned squash whose cooked flesh resembles strands of spaghetti.

**Stock:** a savoury liquid made by simmering aromatic vegetables, herbs, spices, bones and meat or fish trimmings in water.

**Streusel:** a filling or topping for desserts, usually made by combining flour, butter, sugar, and sometimes spices and nuts to form coarse crumbs.

**Tarragon:** a strong herb with a sweet anise taste. In combination with other herbs — notably sage, rosemary and thyme — it should be used sparingly, to avoid a clash of flavours. Because heat intensifies the herb's flavour, cooked dishes require an even smaller amount.

**Tapioca:** an easily digestible starch derived from the fleshy root of a tropical plant. Tapioca swells when it is heated in liquid.

**Total fat:** an individual's daily intake of polyunsaturated, monounsaturated and saturated fats. Nutritionists recommend that total fat constitute no more than 35 per cent of the energy in the diet. The term as used in this book refers to the combined fats in a given dish or food.

**Vanilla extract:** pure vanilla extract is the flavouring obtained by macerating vanilla pods in an alcohol solution. Artificial vanilla flavouring is chemically synthesized from clove oil.

**Wheat berries:** unpolished, whole-wheat kernels with a nutty taste and a chewy texture.

**Wheat germ:** the embryo of the wheat kernel, usually separated out in milling. Wheat germ is high in protein and fat. It should be refrigerated after opening because it can turn rancid quickly.

**Wonton wrapper:** a thin dough wrapper, about 9 cm (3½ inches) square, made of wheat flour and egg; it is used to encase spicy fillings of meat, fish or vegetables.

**Yeast, easy-blend:** a recently developed strain of yeast that reduces the amount of time necessary for rising.

**Yogurt:** a smooth-textured, semi-solid cultured milk product made with varying percentages of fat. Yogurt may be frozen with fruit and eaten as a dessert. It can also be substituted for soured cream in cooking or be combined with soured cream to produce a sauce or topping that is lower in fat and calories than soured cream alone. An alternative is to use thick Greek yogurt. This contains 10 per cent fat, as compared to 18 per cent in soured cream.

# Index

# Picture Credits

All photographs in this book were taken by staff photographer Renée Comet unless otherwise indicated:

Cover: James Murphy. 4: top, Steven Biver. 5: centre, Taran Z; bottom, Michael Latil. 10: James Murphy. 17: James Murphy. 24: Steven Biver. 25: Taran Z. 26: James Murphy. 28: Michael Latil. 33: Taran Z. 34: Steven Biver. 36: Michael Latil. 37: Taran Z. 38: Michael Latil. 40: James Murphy. 42: Michael Latil.

43: top, Taran Z; bottom, Andrew Cameron. 44: left, Taran Z. 49, 50: Steven Biver. 51: Michael Latil. 55: Michael Latil. 59: top, Michael Latil. 64: James Murphy. 67: right, Michael Latil. 73: Steven Biver. 77: top, James Murphy; bottom, Steven Biver. 78: Steven Biver. 80, 81: Steven Biver. 82, 83: Michael Latil. 86, 87: Andrew Cameron. 90, 91: Andrew Cameron. 92: James Murphy. 98, 99: Andrew Cameron. 102: Taran Z. 103: left, Andrew Cameron; right, Taran Z. 106: top, Andrew Cameron; bottom,

Rachel Andrew. 107: Andrew Cameron. 110: Chris Knaggs. 111: left, Chris Knaggs; right, Andrew Cameron. 112, 113: James Murphy. 114: Andrew Cameron. 115: left, Andrew Cameron; right, Taran Z. 118: Andrew Cameron. 119: top, Andrew Cameron; bottom, Chris Knaggs. 120, 121: James Murphy. 124: Taran Z. 125: top, Taran Z; bottom, Chris Knaggs. 126: Michael Latil. 129, 131: Michael Latil. 133: Taran Z. 134-137: Michael Latil.

# Acknowledgements

The editors are particularly indebted to the following people: Jackie Baxter, London; Melanie Barnard, New Canaan, Ct., U.S.A.; Mary Jane Blandford, Alexandria, Va., U.S.A.; Sarah Brash, Alexandria, Va., U.S.A.; Peter Brett, Alexandria, Va., U.S.A.; Denise Cassis, Alexandria, Va., U.S.A.; Shirley Corriher, Alexandria, Va., U.S.A.; Maggie Creshkoff, Pt. Deposit, Md., U.S.A.; Brooke Dojny, Westport, Ct., U.S.A.; Jennifer B. Gilman, Alexandria, Va., U.S.A.; Carol Gvozdich, Alexandria, Va., U.S.A.; Liz Hodgson, London; Rebecca Johns, Alexandria, Va., U.S.A.; Nancy Lendved, Alexandria, Va., U.S.A.; Rebecca Marshall, New York, U.S.A.; Phyllis Paullette, Summit, N.J., U.S.A.; Paula S. Rothberg, Alexandria, Va., U.S.A.; Sarah Wiley, London; CiCi Williamson, Alexandria, Va., U.S.A.; Jolene Worthington, Chicago, U.S.A.; Michele and Michael Sinclair, London.

The editors also wish to thank: Barbara Anderson, U.S. Department of Agriculture, Alexandria, Va.,

U.S.A.; Frank H. Baker and H. C. Palmer, Jr., Nutrition Effects Foundation, Shawnee Mission, Ks., U.S.A.; Joe Booker, Zamoiski Co., Baltimore, Md., U.S.A.; Jo Calabrese, Royal Worcester Spode Inc., New York; Jackie Chalkley, Washington, D.C.; La Cuisine, Alexandria, Va., U.S.A.; Jeanne Dale, The Pilgrim Glass Corp., New York; Rex Downey, Oxon Hill, Md., U.S.A.; Flowers Unique, Alexandria, Va., U.S.A.; Dennis Garrett and Ed Nash, The American Hand Plus, Washington, D.C.; Giant Foods, Inc., Landover, Md., U.S.A.; Judith Goodkind, Alexandria, Va., U.S.A.; Chong Su Han, Grass Roots Restaurant, Alexandria, Va., U.S.A.; Imperial Produce, Washington, D.C.; Oscar Katov, Food Marketing Institute, Washington, D.C.; Kitchen Bazaar, Washington, D.C.; Kossow Gourmet Produce, Washington, D.C.; Gary Latzman and Kirk Phillips, Retroneu, New York; John Lovell, Hayward, Ca., U.S.A.; Magruder's Inc., Rockville, Md., U.S.A.; Micheline's Country French Antiques, Alexandria, Va., U.S.A.; Nambé Mills Inc., Santa Fe,

N.M., U.S.A.; William Nelson, Pacific Tree Farms, Chula Vista, Ca., U.S.A.; Lisa Ownby, Alexandria, Va., U.S.A.; Prabhu Ponkshe, American Heart Association, Washington, D.C.; C. Kyle and Ruth Randall, Alexandria, Va., U.S.A.; Linda Robertson, JUD Tile, Vienna, Va., U.S.A.; Robinson Rainsbottom Pottery Co., Roseville, Ohio, U.S.A.; Safeway Stores, Inc., Landover, Md., U.S.A.; Straight from the Crate, Inc., Alexandria, Va., U.S.A.; Sutton Place Gourmet, Washington, D.C.; United Fresh Fruit and Vegetable Association, Alexandria, Va., U.S.A.; Ann Vaughan, Jenn-Air Company, Indianapolis, Ind., U.S.A.; Williams-Sonoma, Inc., Alexandria, Va., U.S.A. and Washington, D.C.; WILTON Armetale, New York.

*Props for the European edition*: 11: cutlery, Mappin & Webb Silversmiths, London; 26: glassware, Mappin & Webb Silversmiths, London; 92: silverware, Mappin & Webb Silversmiths, London; 121: Wedgwood china, Chinacraft, London.

Typesetting by G. Beard and Son Ltd, Brighton, Sussex, England
Printed and bound by Oriental Press, Dubai